Praise for *The W*

Every now and then I find a work that so ‹
and soul, that I realize that there is a Hom
evolutionary spirituality, for the evolution
seen with evolutionary eyes as coded evolu.... ....
and emergence that helps carry the Impulse of Evolution to full expression and
reality. "The Way of the Wind" by Rev. Bruce Sanguin is such a book. He has
placed the life and meaning of Jesus in the Universal Story of Creation and
seen Him, as I have, as an exemplar of the unrealized potentiality of all of us.
An evolutionary Being of the highest order. The map of Evolution in person. I
believe this book will stand in the Library of Humanity founded by masters such
as Teilhard de Chardin, Sri Aurobindo, John Haught, Beatrice Bruteau, Ilia Delio
to realize that, as Bruce writes:
"A fundamental meaning of the life of Jesus, from an evolutionary perspective,
is that in him, the conditions have been established for the emergence of a
new humanity."
> —Barbara Marx Hubbard, Foundation for Conscious Evolution

One of the key features of the modern world is that we have become, in the
words of Martin Heidegger, "de-worlded", cut off from place, from the earth, from
each other. This book is an antidote to that world. In The Way of the Wind we are
reconnected to the cosmos, to a self which is that cosmos, to the planet, and to
the Divine which runs throughout it all. With a clarity and simplicity of language
Sanguin offers a rich mix of theology, cosmology, evolutionary intelligence and
always practice, a way. When I read this book I just think, "this is the religion, the
spirituality, that I want to partake in during my life". Let the exodus begin.
> — Trevor Malkinson, church planter, United Church of Canada

Sanguin's "evolving mysticism" will challenge both progressives and orthodox
alike - to become ever more human!
> — Rex A E Hunt, Past Chair,
> Common Dreams Conference of Religious Progressives, Australia/New Zealand.

Bruce Sanguin is a gifted spiritual thinker, writer, poet, and mystic. He is one of the few contemporary religious experts who unblinkingly integrates the results of science, especially evolution and cosmology, into a rich and bracing spiritual vision for educated people. This book is proof of that, and it is one to which readers will want to return often.

—John F. Haught, Distinguished Research Professor at the Georgetown University, Theology Dept.

Bruce Sanguin's Jesus and the Evolving Mystic makes a significant contribution to the emergence of evolutionary spirituality. His focus on a mystical approach to a Christian path of love transcends both traditional and progressive versions of Christianity. I was moved throughout the book by Sanguin's own heart of love, which he transmits to the reader in both inspirational and practical terms. Highly recommended.

—Steve McIntosh, author of of *The Presence of the Infinite*, and president of the Institute for Cultural Evolution

Who doesn't want to walk the path of love? Of course plenty of people wonder just what Christianity has to do with it. In a time marked by the church's conflict with science, culture, other religions, and even the dignity of our planet it's easy to just leave Jesus behind. In this book Brucebrings us back to the cosmic, mystical, and consciousness expanding power in Jesus and challenges us to evolve.

—Tripp Fuller, founder of the Homebrewed Christianity Podcast & Director of Theology and the Humanities at Hatchery LA

In the The Way of the Wind Bruce Sanguin has given us a vivid rendering of Evolutionary Spirituality. This lucid and inspired book explores the teachings of Jesus as an invitation to fulfill our evolutionary destiny by becoming ever-more perfect reflections of the singular source. This book has the power to expand and restore your faith. Sanguin has done a service to both Christians and Evolutionaries by outlining a spiritual path that is driven by creative passion, overflowing with love, and softened by an authentic compassion for human frailty.

—Jeff Carreira, author of *The Soul of a New Self: Embracing the Future of Being Human*

The Way of the Wind

Also by Bruce Sanguin:

Summoning the Whirlwind: Unconventional Sermons for a Relevant Christian Faith

Darwin, Divinity, and the Dance of the Cosmos: An Ecological Christianity

The Emerging Church: A Model for Change & a Map for Renewal
(Revised & Expanded)

If Darwin Prayed: Prayers for Evolutionary Mystics

The Advance of Love: Reading the Bible with an Evolutionary Heart

The Way of the Wind

The Path and Practice of
Evolutionary Christian Mysticism

Bruce Sanguin

Viriditas Press, Vancouver

Viriditas Press
3262 West 7th Ave.
Vancouver, B.C. V6K 2A2

Library and Archives Canada Cataloguing in Publication

Sanguin, Bruce, 1955–
The Way of the Wind / Bruce Sanguin.

Includes bibliographical references.
Issued also in electronic format.
ISBN 978-0-9948870-1-6

1. Mysticism--Christianity. I. Title.

BV5082.3.S25 2015   248.2'2   C2015-906588-7

Editor: Editor: Michael Schwartzentruber
Cover and interior Design by Bartosz Barczak
Cover Image: © Yuri Arcurs / iStockphoto

19 18 17 16 15   1 2 3 4 5

To obtain digital or print copies of this book, please visit www.brucesanguin.com.

I believe that the blind-spot which posterity will find most startling in the last hundred years or so of Western civilization is that it had, on the one hand, a religion which differed from all others in its acceptance of time, and of a particular point in time, as a cardinal element of its faith; that it had, on the other hand, a picture in its mind of the history of Earth and man as an evolutionary process; and that it neither saw nor supposed any connection whatever between the two.

—Owen Barfield, *Saving the Appearances: A Study in Idolatry*

Table of Contents

Preface

Forty years of searching for what is real and true draws me back to love, and forward into a future that is being shaped by love. Religious traditions call this Love "God." I'm less concerned with the name we give this Presence than I am in witnessing to it, consenting to it, and ultimately, becoming it, by some grace that is activated only by complete and repeated surrender. I experience this Love as transcendent, yet immanent in this great unfolding we have come to call evolution. This Presence is not "a" person, but is personal, infinitely more personal than whatever we can imagine by the meaning of that term. We emerge from and are being lived by an immense loving intelligence, which manifests in diverse beings, human and non-human. This manifestation is our universe. It is you, the reader, in human form after billions of years of evolution.

Resisting this Love leads to the violence and suffering we now see people enacting toward each other and toward our mother Earth. Surrendering to this Love issues in immense compassion for personal and global suffering, in a deep desire to become one with it and to act on its behalf for a world that is a more perfect reflection of it. To know this Love is to know that there is nothing else really to do with one's life. All else is distraction. Create for love, work for love, raise a family for love, die to oneself for love. This, I know, is not new. Jesus of Nazareth and mystics of every lineage were apprehended by the truth of it. All seekers will come to this awareness in their own time. When we are ready to die to self, Love resurrects us.

I am persuaded that the evolutionary process itself is a great tide of love and that each of us finds fulfillment as we allow ourselves to be swept up in its current. In so doing, we consciously participate in the perfection or the completion of Love. For me, Jesus' core mission was to open our species up to a transformation of love. I believe that his crucifixion was a shamanic act of love, by which everything that was not love was drawn from the world and made to die with him on the cross. His death was a continuation of his ministry of exorcism, by which everything that does not belong (everything that is not love) is drawn out. He died as he lived, drawing out evil, violence, and ignorance, and transforming it with love. The story of the resurrection is an affirmation of the triumph of love and light.

This is all a great mystery, "hidden since the foundation of the world." I do not think that either the evangelical or the progressive Christian church is doing a particularly good job of stewarding this mystery. Many evangelical churches have failed to take the worldviews of modernity and postmodernity seriously enough. The progressive church, on the other hand, has unconsciously taken both worldviews too seriously, to the point that a robust spiritual worldview – grounded in the direct experience of Love – has been sacrificed. The materialistic ideology of the modernist worldview (reducing all of reality to physical reality) is too often uncritically accepted. The relativist (all truth and all values are equal), constructivist (reality is absolutely constructed, not revealed), and "perspectivalist" (there is no truth, just perspective) assumptions of philosophical postmodernism have created a crisis of spiritual confidence.

While I was more identified with liberal or progressive Christianity throughout my 30 years of congregational ministry, I have no commitment at this point in my life to the church as it now exists. I realize that this book is being written as an outsider, hopefully in love, as a provocation to both evangelicals and progressives.

My theology has simplified over the decades. In a nutshell, we are being transformed by and for love. If an emergence of a new kind of human being is underway (which I believe is the case), she will be one who has been emptied of everything that is not love. The resurrection is the story of the birth of the new human. What is asked of us is to enter into a condition of deep consent, what the ancient religious traditions called surrender. Even this emptying is a response to Love living us. We are called to undergo this emptying rather than "make it happen."

At present, humans are living with and are shaped by immense trauma – personal, cultural, and historical. This has made us very dense energetically and has separated us from both our own essential nature, and the nature of the Love that is active in our awakening. This separation is the cost of trauma, from Source, Earth, each other, and self. What we call the personality is only partly temperament. Mostly, it is trauma that has been driven, necessarily, into the unconscious in order for us to survive. The personality (or ego) is then driven by this unconscious trauma. This trauma creates our life, and our social, political, and economic institutions. Until this is all brought to the light of consciousness, we will not be able to create, personally or collectively, from our essential nature or soul. And our essential nature is love. The inability to live from this essence itself becomes the source of ongoing trauma and violence, passed on through our families, and our social, political, and economic institutions.

This drawing forth of all that is not love is the key to the evolution of love in our species. The Christian tradition has called this practice purgation. We tend to associate the word and the practice with self-denial and masochistic practices, like flagellation in the Middle Ages. This is a misunderstanding born of a mistaken belief in the depravity of the human being – the belief that there exists an unbridgeable chasm between G_d's essential goodness and our essential badness (which, according to this false belief, needs to be punished). What is being referred to in this belief is the impact of trauma, which perpetuates personal and systemic violence. But when we are purged of the trauma, our soul comes back on line, and we discover a depth of self-love and love for the world that is our true nature, our Christ-nature.

For some time, readers of my work and those who have attended my talks have asked me which book summarizes my thinking. This is the book I would have referred them to had I been able. In this book, I have attempted to make explicit the underlying thinking and perspectives that have shaped my previous books.

While I have a certain ambivalence about the church at this point in my life, I continue my love affair with that animating presence the church has called "the Christ." This presence was living in, through, and as Jesus of Nazareth, whose teaching we have yet to unpack fully as a species. This is because we cannot understand these teachings until we ourselves have died and been reborn. I maintain that the Christ presence permeates all of creation, Earth, her creatures, you and me, and is implicit in the evolutionary pulse of the universe. This is the cosmic Christ that Paul intuited.

With other mystics, such as Pierre Teilhard de Chardin, I am persuaded that this Christ presence is the fire of love animating the cosmic, biological, and human urge for self-transcendence, and that we are being drawn by this Love that also exerts a pull from an ideal future. This pull is directly accessible when we engage in the practice of transforming the insatiable desire of our traumatized self (ego) into holy longings and following these longings to the divine heart.

In my book The Emerging Church: A Model for Change and a Map for Renewal (Revised Edition), I identified eight core agreements that a community could employ to create a habitat of creative emergence (or evolution). In Chapter Nine of this book, you'll find practices associated with those agreements. The whole field of evolutionary spirituality is a new one and those who are attempting to articulate it are very much in the early stages of identifying practices.

Little of what I write about here is original. Intrinsic to evolutionary spirituality is a humility born of the truth that we are quite literally standing on the shoulders of giants – star fields, solar systems, animating intelligences, an incredible diversity of species – mineral, plant, animal and human – along with ancestral lineages. All these intelligences have shaped us and this immense collective intelligence – what Paul called "the great cloud of witnesses" – is always being drawn from. Among the human giants who have supported me and who continue to support me, I am grateful for Jesus of Nazareth, Paul of Damascus, Johann Wolfgang von Goethe, Rudolph Steiner, Owen Barfield, Teilhard de Chardin, Sri Aurobindo, Evelyn Underhill, Walter Wink, Henri

Bortoft, Brian Swimme, Ken Wilber, Barbara Marx Hubbard, and John Haught. I thank my beloved partner, Mia Kalef, for being such a consistent provocateur for the evolution of love in my own life. I thank my editor, Mike Schwartzentruber, and my book designer, Bartosz Barczak for their acumen.

ONE

Evolution

*The coming of a spiritual age must be preceded by the appearance
of an increasing number of individuals who are no longer satisfied
with the normal intellectual, vital, and physical existence of man,
but perceive that a greater evolution is the real goal of humanity
and attempt to effect it in themselves, to lead others to it,
and to make it the recognized goal of the race.
In proportion as they succeed and to the degree to which they carry this evolution,
the yet-unrealized potentiality which they represent
will become an actual possibility of the future.*
— Teilhard de Chardin

This book began as a short booklet introducing *evolutionary mysticism* as it relates to the lineage of Jesus. It was my way of integrating an experience I underwent during which I realized that there is an essential unity between the cosmos, which has been on a great evolutionary adventure for 13.8 billion years, and my own spiritual journey. Today that adventure continues as we enjoy the immense privilege and responsibility of being the interior dimension of evolution having gained the capacity for conscious evolution: privilege in that we may, in service of the whole creative process up to this point in time, create the ideal conditions for a better future to emerge; responsibility because the freedom conferred upon us by this evolutionary unfolding means that we may also create the conditions that impede or even destroy this evolutionary experiment on Earth. Indeed, unless we soon turn away from the foolishness of the modernist ideology of individualism, and from the economic, social, and political structures that reflect it, we will have failed in our responsibility as a species.

Darwin and love

Before Darwin, theologians, along with German and French philosophers, intuited that we were involved with a developing universe and that this process was being animated by an irrepressible creativity biased toward deeper and more complex expressions of itself. After Darwin, European and North American theologians attempted to make meaning of his discovery. Darwin identified one possible mechanism to describe this force – natural selection (descent with modification), which some have described as one of a handful of great ideas in the history of humanity.

It may come as a surprise to many readers that Darwin himself regarded love, not survival of the fittest, as the most important evolutionary driver in the human realm, and he did not reduce love to biochemistry. He mentions "survival of the fittest twice" in his 828-page book The Descent of Man. Twice! He mentions love 95 times.[1]

> Important as the struggle for existence has been and even still is, yet as far as the highest part of our nature is concerned there are other agencies more important. For the moral qualities are advanced either directly or indirectly much more through the effects of habit, by our reasoning powers, by instruction, by religion, than by "natural selection..."[2]

And this: "But the more important elements for us are love, and the distinct emotion of sympathy."[3]

As modernist scientific consensus crystallized around materialistic assumptions about the nature of reality, Darwin's own writing about love as an

---

1 David Loye, *Darwin's Lost Theory* (Carmel, CA.: Benjamin Franklin Press, 2010), 2.

2 Charles Darwin, *The Descent of Man,* Vol. 2, 1st ed., (London: John Murray, 1879), 404.

3 Darwin, *Descent*, Vol. 49, 2nd ed., (London: John Murray), 524.

evolutionary force simply became invisible to science, despite Darwin's frequent references to love in this regard.

Materialism

Typically, when the word evolution is spoken, what comes to our mind is Darwin, dinosaurs, and DNA. The success of muscular atheists, such as Richard Dawkins, in promoting an exclusively neo-Darwinistic understanding of evolution – for example, that we are driven by selfish genes that are using humans to self-replicate themselves – has contributed to a widespread ignorance about other non-materialistic or spiritual theories of evolution. (The profound irony is that physical bits of genetic material are granted the very will and agency than humans are denied).

All theories coming from the physical sciences about the evolutionary process are concerned, appropriately, with physical reality, and most assume a materialistic worldview – that is, that the world is constituted exclusively of matter and that the "higher" forms of life (such as mind, spirit, soul) are epiphenomena. In other words, somehow matter was their "creator," not G_d, however G_d is understood.

But evolution is not only about physics. It also occurs in the interior realm of consciousness and culture (shared values, beliefs, and assumptions, along with intersubjective relationships), and spirit. When we realize that philosophical materialism is not a scientific conclusion derived from facts, but rather an ideological choice, there is room for theological interpretations of the force that is driving the evolutionary process. There is room, for example, to consider the possibility that the evolutionary drivers themselves evolve over time, so that by the time humans emerge, those drivers have less and less to do with blind chance and more and more to do with the freedom of conscious choice, including the choice to love.

It is this dimension of the evolutionary process that is relevant to a religious or spiritual orientation. And importantly, we need to incorporate consciousness and culture as causative and catalytic factors in the evolutionary process. Consistently, scientists and the public tend to reduce the evolution of consciousness and culture to mere physics, survival of the fittest, and our earliest evolutionary habits of survival.

I imagine the evolutionary process as a divine strategy for birthing and growing a world. This means that "God" (the Originating, Ever-Creative Mystery and the Absolute Potential for Love and Wisdom, hereafter named G_d acknowledging that we will never comprehend this Mystery, even though we can be apprehended by it) acts in and through the evolutionary process in a non-interfering yet persuasive way. Another way of saying this is that G_d so completely pours G_dself into the world that when humans think and act in freedom *for* love and *as* love, they are acting on behalf of G_d. The evolutionary process is an inside job, not the work of a cosmic Engineer, with Source expressing itself through free human beings.

Empathic versus empirical knowing

Science has indeed confirmed that the universe is evolving. Ever since Darwin posited natural selection in 1859 – as mentioned, the still-dominant theory for the mechanism of evolution – every field of science now recognizes that the fundamental nature of reality is evolutionary.[4] Science, however, is concerned with the physical nature of reality, not with making meaning of its findings. The scientific method, which tends to privilege parts over the whole, is one way of knowing the world. But there are other ways.[5]

Prior to the modern, scientific era, empathic knowledge, wherein the knower and the known become one, was the norm. This, indeed, constitutes the mystic path – empathically knowing, uniting with what is known, and thereby awakening to oneness with Reality. Indeed, the reason that we desire so deeply to know the world is that we want to unite with it. Knowing, in its highest form, is a mystical union with the world. Philosophy and theology are two other disciplines by which we come to know the world.

---

4 Alfred Russell Wallace discovered natural selection at the same time as Charles Darwin.

5 For example, Goethe's science of knowing, explicated by philosopher Rudolph Steiner and by Henri Bortoft, represents a wholistic science, or, if you like, a spiritual science.

The making of a world

Unlike some scientists who interpret evolution as nothing more than the meaningless and random collision of atoms which, given enough time, will accidentally come to life and consciousness, I believe that evolution displays purpose and direction. This doesn't mean that there is a single purpose that is being driven by an external G_d. To say that the universe is purposeful does not require us to believe in specific outcomes. We are free creator/creatures directing the course of evolution, at least in relation to our own lives. The future will be formed, therefore, out of our free choices, individually and collectively.

But it is certainly credible to conclude, based on empirical evidence and on our own intuition, that the universe moves in a biased direction toward an increase in complexity (whole becoming parts of larger wholes), unity-in-differentiation, orderliness (which incorporates chaos and randomness), creativity, consciousness, and compassion. These qualities represent the originating and ever-present Heart and Mind pervading the cosmos and human experience, seeking to be materialized, or made physical in a world.

The impulse to evolve, at all scales of reality, is an expression of the fundamental nature of Reality. In humans, this impulse gained the capacity for conscious awareness. All of this is an expression of the impenetrable, ineffable, yet always present Mystery that has been traditionally named "God."

Catholic priest and paleontologist Pierre Teilhard de Chardin summed up the centrality of evolution and why we need to contend with it theologically and experientially in the following way:

> Is evolution a theory, a system or a hypothesis? It is much more: it is a general condition to which all theories, all hypotheses, all systems must bow and which they must satisfy henceforward if they are to be thinkable and true. Evolution is a light illuminating all facts, a curve that all lines must follow.[6]

To reiterate, G_d doesn't engineer or control the evolutionary process. Rather,

6 Pierre Teilhard de Chardin, *The Phenomenon of Man* (New York: Harper and Row, 1955), 218.

G_d "makes" a world that can make itself. Again this "making" need not be thought of as being performed by a Being separate from the world. Rather, using metaphors from quantum physics, the world and G_d are "entangled" (Erwin Schrodinger) in a complementary relationship (Neils Bohr). Entanglement refers to an experiment showing that when two subatomic particles interact, the spin of each can be measured. It turns out that it doesn't matter how far the distance is between these two particles. Once one particle "spins" one way, the other particle will, in complementary fashion, spin in the opposite direction. They are entangled.

Einstein found this "spooky" because it contradicted Newtonian laws of physics – the interaction occurred instantaneously, despite vast distances, contradicting the scientific finding that nothing can move faster than the speed of light. It revealed a universe, which, at the quantum level, is radically interconnected and relational. Psychologist Peter Todd calls this the "internalist perspective," affirming that evolution is an inside job.

Mathematician and philosopher Charles Sanders Pierce (1839–1914) postulated that evolution proceeds through the interplay between purpose and chance. Chance means that there is genuine spontaneity and novelty at play. Over long periods of time, spontaneous occurrences behave more habitually, so much so that they can be termed "laws of nature" by science, which hold particularly at the inorganic level. But even at the large-scale structure of the universe, he proposed that spontaneity pervades the universe. This flies in the face of the deterministic assumptions of much science, philosophy, and theology in our era.[7]

Where intelligent design went wrong

The other form of determinism could be called the argument from God's will or "intelligent design." This is the belief that everything is unfolding ac-

---

7 I concur with Rudolph Steiner, who understands that one cannot apply the same "laws of nature" at the organic, late organic, and human level, for at these stages of evolution, greater degrees of freedom enter the scene, with the effect that life is not merely acted upon, but rather becomes an actor, driven from within (and not externally caused).

cording to a preordained blueprint established by a Super Being external to the cosmos. But there is no preordained blueprint or future that G_d has already planned. This would be a denial of freedom and therefore a denial of the dignity of creation, including, but not limited to, humans.

Pure chance would be absolute randomness and chaos. Pure purposiveness would be blind determinism and render freedom meaningless. The metaphor of "dance" implies that there is an element of randomness and chaos, at all levels and scales of creation that enables the emergence of actual novelty. Chance (or contingency) in the large-scale structure of the cosmos is therefore a precondition for what in the human realm we call freedom. The "laws" of nature (understood as the habits that form after spontaneous and novel eruption, as outlined above) suggest purpose. There is predictability and order in the universe, which science can measure – at least at the scale of large bodies. At the quantum level things get less predictable.

With Todd, we could say that archetypal patterning is woven into the fabric of the universe. Todd looks to quantum physics and Jungian archetypes (particularly the Self archetype) for the foundation of this internalist perspective. Both are examples of what science calls "information" – the mystery by which process comes into formation, or what Christians would call "incarnation" (the Logos or creative principle becoming flesh).

Information is invisible, non-coercive, without mass or energy, and yet active and influential. Information, in the form of quantum processing and archetypal patterning, constitutes what physicist David Bohm calls the "implicate order." Information implies mind, even at the most fundamental levels of life. The universe simply comes equipped with it. It is not an epiphenomenon (emerging out of matter), but rather the cosmic milieu. Mind is what enables the cosmos at all scales to self-regulate, self-organize, and self-renew, and to do so with staggering intelligence, before a human brain ever shows up on the cosmic scene. (Mind here can be distinguished from conscious self-awareness that has evolved in humans and perhaps in a few other mammals.)

Theologian John Haught also sees information as a possible analogy for how G_d is at work in the world. Information holds the purposive end of the polarity, while chaos and unpredictability hold the chance end. It is this creative tension or dance between the two that underlies the creative advance of the universe.

Evolution as drama

Haught encourages us to think of evolution as a drama. A story has a beginning, a middle, and an end. In the middle, all kinds of accidents, including tragedy, keep the narrative unpredictable, and therefore interesting. Some atheistic scientists conclude that the presence of contingency (unpredictability) is the strongest argument *against* G_d. Surely a world that is not perfectly engineered is evidence of "His" absence. Doesn't this rule out G_d? Or if there is a God, "He" is cruel, uncaring, or impotent, or some combination of all three.

Actually, I agree. If there is "a" G_d who could have stopped the holocaust and chose not to, I'm not interested. But if G_d exercises power only as love, not as domination, then G_d is not free to intervene episodically to change the course of history.

Ironically, fundamentalist Christians have this in common with atheistic scientists: they make their case for G_d by claiming that G_d *is* the Great Designer, and then try to use science (poorly) to prove intelligent design. They look for evolutionary gaps, or for aspects of the physical world that they claim are too complex for a random, evolutionary process to produce (for example, the eye), as proof that G_d, not evolution, is at work. Similarly, the presence of evil and suffering are rationalized by the claim that G_d's ways are not our ways, and everything that happens is the direct result of G_d's will. Try telling that to a mother of a young daughter who has died from cancer.

But G_d doesn't control outcomes. A world that was perfectly engineered would be a very boring world. Perfection is static. There's nowhere to go because it's already perfect. We share this planet with other creatures who are, technically speaking, perfect (as in completed). What I mean is that for all their beauty, elegance, and intelligence, they have reached their evolutionary potential. No dog, including my own loving puppy, is sitting around wondering what new life he is being called to live. Dogs are complete.

Humans, on the other hand, will *never* reach their potential precisely because they are also *creators*. Our imperfection, paradoxically, is precisely our particular glory.

Embryologist Jaap van der Wal draws upon research that shows that even as embryos we are unique, in that our movements are not only directed toward Earth, like those of other animals, but also stretch up toward the heavens. This embryonic movement of the human is a patterning, a gesture, suggesting that to the extent that we remain turned only toward Earth, without completing the rhythmic movement toward the heavens, we will not realize the *imago Dei* (image of G_d) within us – creature/creators who will never be finished evolving, never be finished completing both divine incarnation and human potential.

An imperfect, evolving world is an adventure – just like a good story. A better way to think about G_d, therefore, is as storyteller, and the world is a dramatic unfolding of that story. Accidents, dead ends, and all manner of spontaneous eruptions drive the drama. We stay involved precisely because we don't know how it ends.

In fact, this is a story that we ourselves are involved in shaping (not unlike participatory dramas at fringe festivals, when the audience is invited co-create the play as it develops). But the evolutionary story is sustained by the promise of an ending that makes it all coherent and satisfying, and that reflects our deepest intuition of a Wholeness that is living this evolutionary process. The promise is not a slam dunk, however. Even so, we are the creatures who are able to increase the possibility of the fulfillment of that promise through conscious participation in evolving the future.

Theologian and novelist Fred Buechner wrote about the dramatic nature of the gospel as comedy, tragedy, and fairy tale.[8] The thematic threads I've already mentioned – a tendency toward wholeness, creativity, orderliness, and consciousness – provide the fairy-tale dimension of the cosmic narrative.

---

8 Frederick Buechner, *Telling the Truth: The Gospel as Comedy, Tragedy, and Fairy Tale* (San Francisco: Harper & Row, 1977).

These threads give the narrative both coherence, hope, and an intimation that the promise will be fulfilled. The promise of a meaningful ending is embedded throughout the narrative, in our deepest experiences of love and justice. This doesn't mean, however, that we can ignore the tragic dimension of the evolutionary process, which shows up at the cosmic scale as cataclysmic explosions of supernovae, in the realm of nature as extinctions, and in the human realm as the reality of sickness, natural catastrophes, accidents, and evil acts. This tragic dimension is woven into the fabric of the Wholeness that is living us.

The promise

We will see that the theme of G_d's promise is central to scripture. In the meantime, nobody (including G_d) knows how the story ends. But the promise of G_d is that even with all of its imperfection, suffering, and tragedy, the story will be meaningful, fulfilling, and ultimately a story of Love's progress. The ten-dollar name for this in theology is *eschatology*, or *eschatological hope*, and an evolutionary worldview is intrinsically hopeful. Why?

It is hopeful because, in an evolutionary worldview, the presence of crisis evokes the new intelligences necessary to transcend the crisis. In this paradigm, the crisis is also often (but not always) the new birth. Out of the death of a star of sufficient size an explosion occurs, and in the heat of that explosion all the heavy elements necessary for life on Earth (and for you to be reading this) are forged.

We have seen that evolution is a dynamic unfolding of the universe that encompasses all realms of reality – physical, mental, cultural, and spiritual. While much of science reduces evolution to the physical, we do not need to accept this ideological choice. Furthermore, when the evolutionary process reaches the human being, the evolutionary driver can no longer be reduced to mere physics and historical causation. Love enters the playing field. The Source and End of this love is G_d, and has been implicate all along in the evolution of matter into life, of life into conscious self-awareness, and of conscious self-awareness to an inner conviction that the purpose of the whole process is to realize the very heart of the divine. We will explore this as it relates to the Judeo-Christian lineage in the next chapter.

——— TWO ———

Scripture and Evolution

Christ is the evolver, the centrating energy of the evolutionary movement.
But Christ cannot be the energy of evolution unless the incarnation is allowed
to be continued in us.
— Ilia Delio

Jesus' life, death, and resurrection
as the archetypal pattern

In this chapter, I want to apply an evolutionary worldview within the context
of the archetypal patterning displayed in the narrative of the life, death, and
resurrection of Jesus of Nazareth. This narrative constitutes what is sometimes called the "Christ Mystery," with the proviso that we distinguish between the Christ and Jesus (more on this below). By calling it "archetypal" I
mean to imply that this narrative was never meant as something we should
merely "believe." Rather, it was always intended to be a pattern of life that
we participate in. The pattern of Jesus' birth, life, death, and resurrection is
meant to be the archetypal pattern for the community that gathers in his
name. From an evolutionary perspective, when we *do* consciously participate
in his life as our own, we evolve towards a fuller and deeper expression of
what it is to be human.

The early church made the claim that all the pre-existing narratives of
god/humans who incarnate, die, and are reborn (found in the mystery schools
of Egypt and Greece) were enacted *historically* in Jesus. The teachings of the

mystery schools, revealed publicly in Jesus, may indeed be what Paul and the gospel writers referred to as the "mystery hidden since the foundation of the world" (Matthew 13:35, Ephesians 3:1–6). This mystery, which could only be revealed through the secret initiation rituals of these mystery schools, was now made public in Jesus' life, and by believing and participating in Jesus' life, one could be *publicly* initiated into the gnosis (direct knowing) that the mystery schools once performed and provided secretly. This, according to an interpretation of philosopher and esotericist Rudolph Steiner, enabled the "good news" of the great Mystery to be universally accessible – the first sign of which was Paul's realization that the Gentiles were now to be included into what was essentially a Jewish movement.[1]

We can use the Christ mystery revealed in the scriptural narrative, the life and teachings of Jesus of Nazareth, and in the letters of Paul as an interpretive lens that may reveal the deeper meaning of the process and trajectory of evolution. In this section, I will offer a brief overview of how each of these sources can be interpreted from an evolutionary perspective. We will see that although Jesus, Paul, and the biblical writers could not have known about evolution as it is understood today, it is possible to discern within these ancient writings an intuition that everything is moving, animated by the mind of Wisdom, and that this intelligent motion is moving on a biased trajectory, that is, purposively. Using theological language, we can say that G_d is both *within* this process and out in front, as the alluring presence of Love.

Again, it is important to say that we can embrace the scientific discovery of evolution without accepting the materialistic assumptions of some its modernist interpreters. This embrace of science also allows us to interpret tradition doctrine, and scripture, through the lens of evolutionary science. Both science and theology hold interpretive keys that may potentially unlock deeper meanings within these two different ways of knowing reality.

---

1 Rudolph Steiner, *Christianity as Mystical Fact* (Great Barrington, Mass.: Steiner Books, 2006).

The "Old" Testament and evolution

The Jewish scriptures (the "Old" Testament) would have profoundly influenced Jesus' understanding of G_d's will for his life. The core narratives that tell the story of G_d's relationship with the Jewish people over time are unique among the scriptures of the world's religions in their implicit affirmation that history is going somewhere. Unlike the sacred myths of tribal and agricultural societies, which were shaped by the annual cycle of the seasons, Hebrew theology was shaped more by the image of a journey.[2] But the distinctive feature of Judaism was how the Jews were convinced that G_d was accompanying them through history, alluring them covenantally, with the promise of a more abundant life. G_d was going ahead of them, leading them into a promised future and meeting them in the present with intuitions and glimpses of this promise. History was not something to be escaped, as some Eastern religions propose, but rather to be inhabited more deeply in accordance with divine wisdom. In doing so, the people of G_d participated in the realization of the divine promise.

Once one assumes the reality of an evolutionary impulse, the irrepressible forward momentum of the biblical narrative becomes unmistakable. In the Genesis creation myth, the first couple is cast out of the state of perfection in the Garden of Eden. In this paradise there is nowhere to go; after all, it's perfect. But when they are cast out, they enter history, the realm in which to *be* is to *become*, with all of the attendant sufferings that are mentioned in the Genesis story.

Abraham and Sarah are called by G_d to leave home for an adventure in and toward the promise of G_d. The Hebrew people are led out of slavery, G_d going *before* them in a cloud by day and in a pillar of fire by night so that they may realize the promise of freedom. The entire story of the patriarchs from Isaac through to Joseph is a drama that is animated by the pull of a divine

---

2 We need to acknowledge that the liturgical practices of Jews and Christians incorporate and re-interpret these nature festivals that are based in a cyclical view of reality. It also needs to be said that this incorporation, shamefully, was often done with violence, and with the expressed intent of eliminating these cultures and their "idols."

promise. Jacob wrestles with G_d and receives a new name, "Israel" – one who has striven with G_d and has prevailed. Moses is called by G_d to liberate the Hebrew people. This calling causes him to grow beyond his comfort zone, a common theme in the scripture.

Prophets are called to confront kings and queens. Jonah is, against his every instinct, to go to the Ninevites with an offer of divine mercy. Throughout the narrative, G_d calls G_d's people to *be* more; to *risk* more; and to take their next, best step in and toward the divine promise – often in the midst of great resistance. We can see at work here a power that shows up as an urgent, evolutionary impulse to transcend present circumstances, a power that apprehends people as an as-yet-unrealized future.

G_d is not only within the historical impulse to evolve, but also in the pull of the future. John Haught imagines G_d as "The Future."[3] G_d is the realm of infinite possibilities, needing us to make those possibilities real, that is, to actualize them. Faith, as Paul Tillich offered, is being apprehended by the future that comes to meet us in the experience of hope and promise. The future, in this sense, is not tomorrow or even 1,000 years hence. It is the *highest possibility* that can be realized in the present. As such, it is possible to live the future now – as did Jesus.

Living with hope is about co-creating the future that we've glimpsed as that better, self-transcendent possibility. In traditional theology, G_d rules from *up above*. In evolutionary theology, G_d *leads* us from *up ahead*. We are animated by a promise that needs us in order to be realized. Living in faith and hope means becoming agents of conscious evolution, as co-creators of a divine promise.

In the Hebrew scriptures, we can track the evolution of the covenant between G_d and the people. From the covenant with Noah (to not destroy the world), to the Abrahamic covenant (to make Abraham the father of a great nation) to the Mosaic covenant (the moral code of the Ten Commandments), we see an implicit evolution of what it means to be a holy people, set apart, not

---

3 Following theologians Jürgen Moltmann and Wolfhart Pannenberg.

for privilege, but to be a light unto the nations. The covenant with Jeremiah, in which the law will be written upon the hearts of the people and will therefore require no teachers, represents the evolution of freedom. A holy people are not determined by external laws, nor is obedience to external authority the highest form of spiritual law. Rather, to know directly, through a mystical knowing, how to act in freedom, in and for love, reflects the heart of G_d.

The New Testament and evolution

The New Testament is the story of Jesus' life contained in the gospel accounts, and the early church's interpretation of his life contained in Paul's letters. With Jesus of Nazareth as our primary exemplar, we look at his life as a template for where this divine impulse to evolve a world is headed. In this sense, we read back, from the story of his life, death, and resurrection, and from his teachings, to the origins of the universe – the Big Bang – and imagine that his love and wisdom is a manifestation of the divine Mind and Heart out of which a universe emerged, is sustained, and is evolving. He represents, in human form, the fulfillment of the promise inherent in the Big Bang. He is a new creation, as Paul says, and today we could say a new Big Bang, in human form.

We also read *forward* from his life to a promised future. For Christians, Jesus is a down payment on the future promise.

This is what it means to affirm that Jesus is "the Christ." Christ is a title, not Jesus' last name. It means *anointed*. Jesus was anointed, through his own conscious willingness, to be a radiant expression of the Heart and Mind of G_d. His love, his compassion for the other (including the "enemy"), and his commitment to establishing G_d's realm (Kin(g)dom of G_d) on Earth is an expression of the purpose of this evolving universe that took 13.8 billion years to manifest. Jesus was completely transparent to the G_d, whose presence can be felt as the urge within the evolutionary impulse, beckoning from the realm of future possibilities.

In the prologue of John's gospel, Jesus is presented as the Word made flesh. "The Word" is a translation of the Greek word *logos*, which in Greek philosophy is the creative principle. Scholars such as Elizabeth Johnson identify this creative principle with Sophia, the feminine divine, who is co-creator and architect of the world with G_d. This creative principle, says the author of John, is what became flesh in Jesus of Nazareth. For me, the Christ is the principle of creative transformation, personalized in Jesus after 13.8 billion years, but also in all who now consciously choose to be agents of G_d's promise for a more beautiful, good, and true world.

The whole of creation, not only Jesus, is the manifestation of this creative principle, whether we call it Wisdom, the Word, or non-religiously as the evolutionary current that fashions a universe of increasing complexity. Jesus, for Christians, is what a human being becomes when s/he completely surrenders to being lived by this sacred current of creativity. This is the Christ Mystery, this incarnational dynamic that constitutes reality and that was also revealed in Jesus of Nazareth, whom some Christians refer to as "the" incarnation.

A fundamental meaning of the life of Jesus, from an evolutionary perspective, is that, in him, the conditions have been established for the emergence of a new humanity. The universe can now *do* a Jesus, and therefore it becomes possible that the same Mind and Heart that animated him is available to us. This we will see is critical for a mystical practice. Jesus "gave himself for us" in the sense that he laid down the evolutionary grooves for the emergence of a new kind of human. And this is what the stories of the resurrection confirm – that a new human has been raised, and that we are being raised, with Jesus, to the condition of a new humanity. The process of our own becoming, consciously embraced, is the process of realizing our deep humanity as spiritual beings.

Jesus' teaching picks up the theme of promise from the Old Testament. The metaphor that Jesus uses to express this promise is not the "promised land," but rather the kin(g)dom of G_d. I've bracketed the (g) in recognition of the empirical truth that we are of one lineage with all of creation: the stars, gases, minerals, elements, plants, creatures, etc. We are kin in the kin(g)dom of G_d.

The kin(g)dom of G_d is what our personal lives would look like if love and not ego reigned; it is what our relationships would look like if we loved others as we love ourselves (that is, as G_d loves us); it is what our collective life would look like socially, economically, and politically if G_d's passion for justice and peace reigned in our systems; and finally, it is what our relationship with Earth would look like if we grasped our essential interconnectedness with Earth. The kin(g)dom of G_d is a realm of no-separation. When the illusion of separation from the cosmos, from Earth, creation, each other, and G_d falls away, we are being lived by this mysterious, unitive realm of Wholeness. The Wholeness (G_d) is in the process of realizing itself, through a universe that is becoming.

Jesus is distinguished by the fact that he was able to see this Wholeness in others, particularly in the marginalized and the ill, when others could only see castoffs. He saw the Wholeness everywhere, despite living in a world that was fragmented, and in his way of seeing and acting he *was* the kin(g)dom of God in the flesh, the future present.

The kin(g)dom of G_d is always already present and yet also waiting to be realized through our conscious cooperation with the divine impulse to evolve, through our conscious consent to surrender to the call of G_d to go beyond our comfort zone and to take responsibility for the realization of G_d's preferred future – personally, relationally, and corporately. It is the future waiting to be realized now, as we drop into a condition of non-separation and gain a mystical vision of the primordial Wholeness underlying the apparent brokenness and alienation of the world. Again, this future is not tomorrow or next month. It is our highest possibility today.

This primordial Wholeness (G_d) is the health of creation and is always, everywhere present. When we align ourselves with the coherence of love and wisdom, the future that emerges in and through our co-creative presence manifests the Kin(g)dom of G_d.

Jesus teaches that the proper orientation of his followers is the future (again, understood as the highest possibility for us *today*). "Anyone who puts [her] hand to the plough and looks back is not fit for the kin(g)dom (realm) of G_d." There is no excuse for delay, not even the moral and spiritual obligation to bury one's own father (Matthew 8:22). This is surely hyperbole, a favourite rhetorical device of Jesus. Nevertheless, you can feel the sense of urgency to "press on" (Philippians 3:14), to render as relative all that would keep one from the absolute importance of the vocation of revealing and realizing the kin(g) dom of G_d. In the call of the disciples, this sense of urgency is captured as, one by one, they leave everything to follow him. Today this call may be interpreted as the evolutionary urgency to consciously evolve our species in the hope of ensuring a future for generations of life on Earth.[4]

This forward-looking orientation of Jesus also relates to our modern tendency to focus on misery, evil, and injustice. It's not that these things aren't real; they are. But without the deep-time perspective of an evolutionary worldview, we lack sufficient perspective to contextualize evil within a life process that privileges an increase in beauty, truth, and goodness. Jesus may have been informed by the story of Lot's wife looking back upon the burning city of Sodom. She has become transfixed by the evil of the city, and upon looking back she is turned into a pillar of salt. We need to take evil seriously and challenge it. But when we focus exclusively on evil, we may inadvertently be joining Lot's wife. In evolutionary terms, she devolves; she literally returns to an earlier stage of evolution that got as far as minerals.

I have long felt that many forms of progressive Christianity with good intent are nevertheless more transfixed by evil and injustice than by the joy, beauty, and goodness of creation. The divine promise in both the first and second (Old and New) testaments does not ignore injustice, but the end point is the city of G_d. It is my experience that evolutionary spirituality and theology issue in a realistic hopefulness.

New wineskins

Jesus began many of his teachings with the phrase, "You have heard it said... but I say unto you," indicating that his was a new teaching. His intention was

---

4 It is important to note that this future orientation need not exclude the wisdom of the past, particularly indigenous wisdom. In fact, the modernist disassociation from the indigenous sensibility of directly participating in the intelligence of the universe is something that Christians need to re-collect and incorporate. This same wisdom informs the mystic orientation.

to evolve the tradition by breaking open his lineage to new depths and new interpretations. He taught that one cannot put new wine into old wineskins, because the new wine will burst the wineskins. A new container is required.

Jesus didn't intend to start a new religion. Rather, he wanted to help the tradition evolve, as many Jewish prophets had done before him. To be on the path of Jesus, then, is to take on his spirit, which is continually breaking open and advancing– not replacing – tradition. By interpreting evolution from within this path, and by interpreting our tradition through the lens of evolution, we are being faithful to the spirit of Jesus. It is the very heart of our lineage to watch for how Spirit is moving to evolve the tradition. We will see in a future chapter on "Jesus as nomad" how this nomadic orientation is essential, if we are serious about listening for Spirit.

The metaphor of the seed

One of Jesus' favourite metaphors is the seed, and its mysterious potential to grow and bear fruit. A sower goes out to plant seeds (the Word); a farmer plants seed in the ground and goes to bed. Before long, the farmer knows not how, the seed has mysteriously grown into a plant. Faith is compared to a mustard seed that increases in size and becomes a tree,[5] which provides shelter for the birds. I interpret his teaching in a way that draws our attention to three interrelated dynamics: 1) the growth of a seed describes how G_d's grace works in the universe, from the inside out and within the impulse to become; 2) we ourselves *are* divine seeds; the same natural grace that animates seeds is working within us to bear fruit; and 3) the very image of G_d is within us in potential form, just as an oak is within an acorn in potential form. But when humans focus on exteriors (the husk and not the kernel) we fall into idolatry, confusing the true life within with the shell.

Our spiritual journey involves consciously realizing that potential, which is *our* potential, by allowing a natural grace, an evolutionary impulse, to animate our living. We are the seeds of a new creation, being "informed" by the

---

5 The biblical editor got this detail wrong. Mustard seeds don't grow into trees.

push and pull of the divine to bear distinctive fruit.

The legend of Jesus' birth is also a kind of seed story. Mary is invited by an angel to receive and gestate the divine seed of the Holy Spirit. This can be interpreted as the early church's way of undermining Empire's claim that G_d privileges rich and powerful men. By imagining that Mary's conception happens directly from G_d's seed, another oppressive institution – patriarchy – is bypassed and undermined. Divine birth occurs outside the patriarchal "norm" of male privilege. In the words of Canadian singer-songwriter Bruce Cockburn, "Mary has a child without the help of a man." In this birth story, a new order breaks in upon the existing order of death. In this birth, the evolutionary way forward is revealed in "future shining in a baby's eye."[6] In these ways, the story of Jesus' birth symbolizes the divine intention for the evolution of our species. By inference, to follow Jesus means committing our lives to the evolution of our social, political, and economic systems.

I've mentioned that scientific materialism reduces all of reality down to matter, and that organic life, mind, and whatever we mean by soul are merely epiphenomena, that is, *products* of matter. But this is untenable for a spiritual worldview. A principle of the perennial philosophical tradition is that the lower cannot give birth to the higher. But it is possible for the higher dimensions, or you could say the more subtle dimensions, to emerge out of the lower. This becomes possible if we assume that the more subtle and more complex levels of reality are hidden, latent within matter. As the kernel is hidden within the outer husk of a seed, so within matter is the kernel of mind and life. Within life is the kernel of consciousness, and within consciousness is the kernel of conscious self-awareness. And all of this is being lived by Spirit. I believe this is why the seed metaphor, with the germ being concealed within a shell that must die, was so important for Jesus. It shows or illustrates the true relationship between matter, life, mind, and spirit.

The great Indian philosopher Sri Aurobindo puts it this way, using the teaching of the Vedanta lineage:

---

6 Bruce Cockburn, "The Cry of a Tiny Babe," on *Nothing But a Burning Light* (Golden Mountain Music, 1991).

We speak of the evolution of Life in Matter, the evolution of Mind in Matter; but evolution is a word which merely states the phenomenon without explaining it. For there seems to be no reason why Life should evolve out of material elements or Mind out of living form, unless we accept the Vendantic solution that Life is already involved Matter and Mind in Life because in essence Matter is a form of veiled Life, Life a form of veiled Consciousness. And then there seems to be little objection to a farther step in the series and the admission that mental consciousness may itself be only a veil of higher states which are beyond Mind. In that case, the unconquerable impulse of man toward God, Light, Bliss, Freedom, Immortality presents itself in its right place, chain as simply the imperative impulse by which Nature is seeking to evolve beyond Mind...[7]

Jesus uses two other images that can describe how evolution works from a spiritual perspective. He uses the images of the seed, but also of leaven and buried treasure, I believe, to describe this mystery by which the more complex and more subtle is hidden within the less complex. Leaven is invisible in the bread and yet causes it to rise and become something that it would not have been without its presence. Matter in this sense contains the buried treasure. Quantum physics indeed is revealing that matter is comprised mostly of space and this space is not empty or inert. A potent, fecund dimension of life is hidden within matter.

All three images suggest the dynamic of emergence. Under the right conditions, there is a mysterious force at work in the universe from which, by the attraction and communion of two different elements, something completely unpredictable and novel, (which cannot be reduced to either part nor to the sum of the parts) emerges. Nobody could have predicted the emergence of life out matter, of consciousness out of life, or of soul out of conscious awareness. Science certainly cannot explain it. What we are dealing with here is the reality that the Whole is already, always present in each part waiting for the right con-

---

7 Sri Aurobindo, *The Life Divine* (Twin Lakes, WI.: Lotus Press, 2000), 7.

ditions in order to emerge in many different forms, and in new expressions of consciousness and culture.

Paul's letters and evolution

Besides the gospels and the book of Acts, the other major portion of the New Testament is comprised of Paul's letters. Seven of these are authentically Pauline,[8] and the others are either disputed or simply attributed to Paul by other writers, a common practice in the first century. Paul is the founder of the church, particularly the Gentile church. In the spirit of the Christ, Paul discerns that he is being called to open grace, and the church itself, to Gentiles. This was very controversial and put Paul at odds with the leaders in Jerusalem, who regarded the church as a new expression of Judaism, with all the attendant rituals and codes of that lineage intact. But Paul was convinced that the promise of G_d was being made available to non-Jews. This would entail letting go of the ancient rituals, purity codes, initiation practices (circumcision), and Sabbath practices that defined Judaism.

For Paul, being "free" in Christ implied letting go of an earlier iteration of faith, relinquishing obedience to an external authority as the basis of the practice of faith, and allowing this new faith to evolve into what he called a "new creation" in Christ. Paul's mission was to enact the radically evolutionary path of Jesus.

A favourite metaphor of Paul was the development from childish spirituality to adult spirituality. For Paul, the Law (and the customs, rituals, and practices of Judaism and Greco-Roman religion) acted like a babysitter until novices attained spiritual maturity and were able to live by the Spirit naturally and organically – until, that is, the love that animated Jesus apprehended and transformed his followers. Then there was no need for external laws.

Paul's understanding of the Law (Torah) evolved. He was so filled with the love of Christ, and with the impulse to be an agent of creative transformation, that his actions organically reflected this imperative. He needed no

---

8 Galatians, Philemon, 1 and 2 Corinthians, Romans, Philippians, and 1 Thessalonians.

external set of laws to control his behaviour. He was set free (Galatians 5:1) for freedom. He was "in Christ." Jeremiah, as we've seen, prophesied in the Old Testament that the law of G_d would be written upon our hearts, and no teachers would be required (Jeremiah 31:33). This was true to such an extent that Paul experienced Christ as the very core of his own identity: "It is no longer I who live, but Christ who lives in me" (Galatians 2:20). This sense that the love of Christ had set him free from external authority is what Paul wanted for every member of the church.

Paul himself underwent a *metanoia*. Typically, this Greek word is translated as "conversion," usually associated with repentance. While this certainly captures the result of *metanoia*, the word itself means "higher mind" (*meta* is higher, and *noia* is mind). Paul was changed completely by having the mind of Christ enter into and lift up his rational mind. He changed from being a violent man, who persecuted the early church, to a man of love, who became the church's most effective proponent. After encountering Jesus in some kind of spiritual body after Jesus' crucifixion, Paul commits his life to building communities of Christ-followers among the Gentiles. He changed his name from Saul to Paul. As we've seen, his understanding of Jewish purity, initiation, and holiness codes also evolves. Circumcision was no longer required as a rite of initiation, and Gentiles would not be required to eat kosher food. This was a dramatic evolution of the tradition and makes sense given that Paul was tapping into the field of Christ consciousness that animated Jesus, and Jesus was first and foremost an evolver of tradition.

For Paul, the death and resurrection of Jesus initiated a new creation. The risen Jesus was the "first fruit" of this new creation, and everyone who had the faith *of* Christ (as distinct from a traditional faith *in* Christ) was also destined to become the new creation. Humanity itself was evolving, in Christ. A new expression of the human species, oriented from an interior dimension, filled with love, gentleness, kindness, humility, and all the fruits of the spirit, was emerging (Galatians 5:22–23). Paul exhorted people to the "let the same mind be in you that was in Christ Jesus" (Philippians 2:5).

The section from Paul's letter to the Corinthians that has been read countless times at weddings sounds, to my ears, explicitly evolutionary. We are meant to evolve from childhood to a mature, adult spirituality of love:

> When I was a child, I spoke like a child, I thought like a child, I reasoned like a child; when I became an adult, I put an end to childish ways. For now we see in a mirror, dimly, but then we will see face to face. Now I know only in part; then I will know fully, even as I have been fully known. (1 Corinthians 13:11–12).

One non-Pauline letter, 1 John, also expresses an evolutionary intuition: "Beloved, we are God's children now; what we will be has not yet been revealed. What we do know is this: when he is revealed, we will be like him, for we will see him as he is" (1 John 3:2).

Like Paul, this writer intuits that while those in the community are now children of G_d, today, there will be a maturing process. Who knows what the future might hold? But, like Paul, he is persuaded that when the Christ Mystery is revealed, "we will be like him." The community of the beloved is evolving, that is *being drawn*, to realize their own Christ-like nature. And this Christ-like nature, in the form of the human being, is not something that is added on. Rather, it is already present, as the oak tree exists in potential within the acorn, waiting to come into its fullness, when conditions are ripe.

Cosmic Christ

One thread of scripture, coming from Paul and from John's gospel, is the idea of the cosmic Christ. In fact, Paul was much more interested in the cosmic Christ than the human Jesus. We know that "Christ" is not Jesus' last name. The Christ is the *Logos* (Word) of John's gospel, who was in the beginning with God, and through whom all things came into being (John 1:2–3). The gospel writer goes on to say, "What has come into being through him was life, and the life was the light of all people. The light shines in the darkness and the darkness did not overcome it" (vss. 5–6).

In chapter eight in John's gospel, the author shows explicitly that he believed that Jesus was the Christ incarnate when we hear Jesus say, "Before

Abraham was, I Am" (John 8:58). The "I Am" phrase identifies Jesus with the Great I Am, God (Exodus 3:14).

It was this creative principle, or what Christian theology has called the second person of the Trinity, that (who) became flesh in Jesus. But it is critical to realize in cosmic Christology that this creative source did not limit itself to Jesus, but rather was present in all "life," and that in the human realm it was the "light of all people" – that is, the cosmic Christ includes but goes beyond Christianity. S/he is present in all creation (all life, inorganic, organic, and human) as the light of God. My book *Darwin, Divinity, and the Dance of the Cosmos: An Ecological Christianity* is, in this respect, an extended reflection on the implications of the theology of the cosmic Christ for ecology.

We could say, with Franciscan priest Fr. Richard Rohr, that the cosmic Christ is born at the Big Bang 13.8 billion years ago, and that the story of our 13.8-billion-year universe is the story of the evolution of the sacred, creative principle manifesting, through evolution, a universe. Everything is therefore sacred.

The birth of Jesus is the story of the birth of the Cosmic Christ in a *particular* human being. This human being incarnated the creative principle (the Christ or the Word) to such a degree that he was identified with the creativity that brought forth a universe. In his very being and presence, he created new worlds, opened up sealed futures, and laid the evolutionary blueprint down for the dawning of a new humanity. To be "raised with Christ" means precisely to become, in and through this Christ-infused evolutionary grace, the new human.

Paul intuited that Jesus was animated by the creativity that brought forth and permeates the entire universe – the Christ principle: "He is the image of the invisible God, the firstborn of creation; for in him all things in heaven and on earth were created, things visible and invisible... – all things have been created through him and for him. He himself is before all things, and in him all things hold together" (Colossian 1:15–17).

Paul understands Jesus as the Christ when he writes, "With all wisdom and insight he has made known to us the mystery of his will, according to his good pleasure that he set forth in Christ, as a plan for the fullness of time, to gather up all things in him, things in heaven and things on earth (Ephesians

1:8–10). He understands Jesus as what I call a concentrated amalgam of the entire universal process, the fruition of a cosmos that has realized itself fully in him. He is also a glimpse or a foretaste of where the universe is going. All things will be gathered up and fully realized, as the universe was gathered up and fully realized in Jesus. Just as Jesus is love incarnate, so all of humanity (and through humans, all creation) will become love.

This creative, loving power (the cosmic Christ), which is animating the evolutionary process and which issued in Jesus of Nazareth, wants to fulfill itself in everything and everybody. This is our *destiny*. Our *vocation* is to allow this grace to have its way with us, that is, to allow ourselves to know the cosmic Christ as a living presence within.

—— THREE ——

Mysticism

The Christian of the future will either be a mystic,
one who has experienced something,
or she will cease to be anything at all.
— Karl Rahner

Many people associate mysticism with New Age "woo-woo" spirituality. But the greatest scientist that ever lived, Albert Einstein, said that the mystical emotion is the highest emotion available to us. In her book *Practical Mysticism*, Anglo-Catholic writer Evelyn Underhill defined mysticism in non-religious terms as "the art of union with Reality," leaving it up to the reader to determine what constitutes reality.

The unitive experience

The "mystical emotion" is grounded in an experience of unity – the awareness and experiential feeling that reality is One, and that we are expressions of that unity manifesting in wondrous diversity. This mystical sensibility that there is one, seamless reality and that we are an expression of that unity is grounded both in science and in the sensibility of mystics of all religious traditions, including Judaism and Christianity.

Science is revealing a universe that supports this mystic intuition. Cosmology is the study of the large-scale structures of the universe. What cosmologists now know is that everything and everybody shares a common origin, the Big Bang. Galaxies, supernova, our solar system, Earth, and every plant, animal, or human that ever emerged came from this Great Radiance 13.8 billion years ago. We are literally made from the same stuff as everything else. All life forms share the same genetic material, amino acids, and building blocks. Our diversity arises from the fact that these materials can be arranged in different ways. The human being is a composite amalgam of 4.5 billion years of life on Earth and 13.8 billion years of cosmic evolution. The whole universe is literally gathered up in us. We are the presence of the universe, in human form, consciously evolving.

Incarnation as mystical experience

It's a bit of a cliché to say that we are the offspring of an exploding star, but that description happens to be empirically accurate. All the heavy elements necessary for the emergence of life on our planet came from exploding stars. It can be stated non-romantically that in our human form we are the reconfigured presence of the original fireball. It just took 13.8 billion years to get to us! Our unity with the cosmos is based in evidence; this is scientific mysticism, not romantic idealism. The 21st century is unique insofar as a growing number people are awakening, for the first time in the history of our species, to the truth that we are the evolutionary process awakening to itself.

The universe explodes into being. Leave it alone, and after 13.8 billion years it becomes aware of itself *in* and *as* you and me. This is a stunning moment, a realization of our "deep-time" identity. It is only in the last 50 years that we have had access to this knowledge. This is a game-changer that no school of wisdom and no religious tradition had known about. We are not separate, lonely individuals, desperate to connect in an isolating and uncaring universe. It's not simply that we belong in the universe. (We do!) It's that we *are* the universe, in human form, evolving. Our belonging is so radical, so deep, that there is no disconnection – anywhere! There is distinction and differentiation, yes. And yes, we may *feel* alienated. But if this is how we feel, then we have lost connection with Reality, with our deep, cosmic identity as the universe in human form. This unity is primal. It took an entire universe, and all this time, to arrive at you, at me, at *us*.

A definition of evolutionary mysticism

And what does the universe want to do? It wants to evolve *through* us, because this is just what the universe does. In us, the universe is able to consciously evolve. In evolutionary mysticism, we imagine that G_d/Spirit *is*, or if you prefer, is *within*, this impulse to evolve, and we are most truly ourselves when we are conscious of this impulse and have the wholehearted intention to be *That* which wants to evolve through us. To be "in Christ," then, is to awaken to this cosmic identity, this Big Self, and to *be* the new creation that needs you/us in order to emerge. The Christian mystic says "yes" to this unity with All That Is, and "yes" to this sacred impulse to be a vessel for the new thing G_d is doing *through* us and *as* us. When we are living out of our deep, unitive, cosmic identity, we are animated by the life of this process; we realize our power; and we understand that nobody else can bring forth the unique future that is ours to manifest.

It is critical in evolutionary mysticism to understand that we are embodied and personalized expressions of this push and pull to evolve – and that we are inspired to do so not merely for our own personal growth, but in service of the evolution of the universe itself. To get this is to experience what futurist Barbara Marx Hubbard calls "vocational arousal." Our lives are not our own, meaning they are not simply for the realization of our personal goals. Our lives are for the realization of the *universal goal* of evolving deeper expressions of what it means to be fully human, fully divine, and fully cosmic. We are the presence of the universe evolving in and toward a divine promise of greater freedom and greater love.

We are the interior dimension of the universe evolving. And this interior dimension is filled with "G_d": the Mind (conscious intelligence) and Heart (love) that is the ground of Being, or the "divine milieu" from which a universe emerged and evolved 13.8 billion years ago and which continues to emerge and evolve. The paradox is that *we are That* which we've been seeking our entire lives. What I mean is that we are embodied expressions of the mystery of the Holy One and of the Sacred Oneness of Reality. Through the cultivation of conscious awareness and loving kindness, we come to realize that, far from being separate from the originating Heart and Mind, we are its most intimate expression.

When Jesus says in John's gospel, "Before Abraham was, I Am," the author is expressing a profound mystery: Jesus is a manifestation of the Great I Amness out of whom a universe emerged. He is the consciousness (Mind) and the love (Heart) of G_d in flesh and blood.

Evolutionary mysticism affirms incarnation – the Mind and Heart of G_d becoming flesh – but not "the" incarnation, where this is interpreted as an event exclusive to Jesus of Nazareth. In other words, incarnation includes "the" incarnation of Jesus, but goes beyond that to include *all* of creation.

The incarnational dynamic of the "the Secret One, slowly growing a body"[1] did not just happen once upon a time, 2,000 years ago in Palestine. Rather, it is the story of the evolution of matter from energy, life out of matter, mind out of life, and conscious awareness out of mind. It is the story of the evolving universe in its exterior (physical) and interior (consciousness and culture) dimensions. We are incarnations of the divine, but so are bacteria, bats, butterflies, and baboons – not to mention galaxies, supernovae, and granite. Earth is indeed filled with G_d's glory (Isaiah 6:6). To awaken to incarnation is to discover the source of our deeply-felt ecological imperative to repair Earth and to walk lightly upon her. Earth truly is the body of G_d.[2]

Because we are embodied creatures who experience suffering, death, and all manner of indignities during our lifespan, we have a tendency to forget our oneness with G_d and cosmos. Like the prodigal son, we wander away from home, confusing our cosmic inheritance – unity with All That Is – with money, or success, or status. We suffer the indignity of the prodigal species as the one creature among all who is imbued with conscious self-awareness but who uses this evolutionary treasure to pursue all that does not satisfy. We squander our inheritance pursuing the desires of the small, personal self. We

---

1 Kabir, "Between the Conscious and the Unconscious," in Stephen Mitchell, *The Enlightened Heart: An Anthology of Sacred Poetry* (New York: HarperCollins, 1973).

2 See my book Darwin, *Divinity, and the Dance of the Cosmos: An Ecological Christianity* (Wood Lake Publishing, 2007).

build society – our educational, social, economic and political institutions – as projections of the illusions of our separate self. This reinforces our feelings of fragmentation and alienation from Source.

The mystic has had the experience of *awakening*, like the prodigal son. In the words of the parable, we "come to our senses," as did the prodigal son. We realize that our wandering off, our existential forgetfulness, was necessary, preliminary, and preparatory to our waking up. We return home with our repentance speech all prepared. But the "father" is not interested in our speech. The father/mother, of course, is the Heart and Mind of the universe, from whom we can never actually be separated. We've come home to the cosmos, home to the Heart of the universe. We were lost, but now we're found. The illusion of separation dissolves. We are always already home. G_d throws her arms around us and welcomes us as though we had never left (which we hadn't!).

Ideally, those who walk in the path of Jesus are a community of evolving mystics who realize their unity with Spirit, cosmos, and Earth, and who seek to live their lives in accordance with this consciousness. In the spirit of Jesus and the church's founder, Paul, these souls recognize that the tradition is always in the process of being broken open to make room for the new thing G_d is doing. The universe is evolutionary in nature. Out of the originating mystery, divine Heart and Mind involves itself with a "world." Thus begins the slow and patient journey of a universe non-coercively realizing a world that is self-aware, that is in the process of manifesting this originating milieu of Love, Intelligence, and Creativity. We *are* that divine process, embodied in human form, evolving. It is an exciting and challenging time to be alive on Earth. It is urgent that we awaken and respond to the divine and cosmic impulse to evolve and to assume responsibility for revealing and incarnating the realm Jesus called the Kin(g)dom of G_d.

This is evolutionary mysticism as it relates to a spiritual community: a community of individuals on the path of Jesus (or Buddha, Mohammed, Krishna, etc.), consciously evolving in community, one with the evolving cosmos and one with the divine Heart and Mind, in loving service to our one

Earth community. The distinctive vocation of the evolutionary mystic is to allow her or himself to be apprehended again and again by the most intimate, intense, and immense future that is possible for that individual or community.

—— FOUR ——

Tenets of Evolutionary Mysticism

To live in an evolutionary spirit means to engage with full ambition
and without reserve in the structure of the present,
and yet to let go and flow into a new structure
when the right time has come.
— Erich Janstsch

1. Evolution is a divine strategy for revealing and realizing (making real) a world that can make itself

Catholic spiritual teacher Richard Rohr says that G_d's first big idea was to materialize. The world emerges from the womb of G_d. We are, everything is, in the provocative images of futurist Jean Houston, "godlings." This again is the mystic sensibility – that our connection with G_d is primordial and direct. What emerges as a cosmos is the body, mind, and heart of G_d, evolving in space and time. Creation is the maturation of the divine.

One of the implications of this worldview is that there is nowhere and no thing that is not intrinsically sacred, because everything is participating in the ongoing emergence or realization of G_d, including but not limited to the human realm. This has obvious ecological implications, which I wrote about in *Darwin, Divinity, and the Dance of the Cosmos*. When we get our identity straightened out as "godlings" and see the world itself to be a manifestation of the divine, we naturally are inclined to walk with reverence upon Earth and to live respectfully. We see creation as more than a "resource" to extract for our purposes.

The world makes itself by participating at every level from sub-atomic particles to human beings in a drive for self-transcendence. Pervading the universe is a dynamic that French Catholic paleontologist Teilhard de Chardin calls "attraction-communion-complexification." As creation follows its allurements (in the human realm through holy longings), communion with the source of the attraction results in complexification.

When philosopher and mathematician A. N. Whitehead wrote that "the many become one and are increased by one," he was referring to this dynamic of self-transcendence. The new thing (the increase of one) that is born of the attraction and communion cannot be reduced to its constituent parts. It is novel. This is emergence, or self-transcendence. And this dynamic is pervasive. Using religious language, it reveals and *is* the work of the Holy Spirit. This dynamism eventuated in the revealing of conscious self-awareness in humans, with the result that we are now able to experience an awakening, or enlightenment, as the realization that we are this process of attraction-communion-complexification-consciousness in the form of humans, and we can choose to consciously participate in it.

The practice is subversively simple: drop into your deepest longings for your life and for your world, and remove every obstacle that is keeping you from organizing your life around these longings. In this way, we awaken to own godling-nature. We gain the freedom to consciously participate in the evolutionary process. We are that part of the world able to *consciously* "make itself." This is both the privilege and the great responsibility of the human being. We are no longer merely determined by the past. We have acquired the capacity to be *determiners* of the future. This represents the emergence of freedom.

To be conscious world-makers is an awesome responsibility. The literary giant Owen Barfield says that this confers upon us a "directionally creator" relationship to the rest of nature, a role in which we are currently failing.[1]

---

1 Owen Barfield, *Saving the Appearances: A Study in Idolatry*, 2nd ed., (Middleton, CT: Wesleyan University Press, 1988), 132.

2. Evolutionary spirituality includes but transcends Darwin, DNA, and dinosaurs

There is a tendency in spiritual lineages to hold the physical realm as lower than, and in some cases *opposed to*, the spiritual. But as cosmologist Brian Swimme points out, only approximately four percent of the universe is comprised of matter. Considering that there are billions of galaxies each with trillions of stars (a lot of matter!) this is quite remarkable. Matter is actually a very rare accomplishment and therefore to be honoured. It is the body of G_d, not the *lowest* level, but rather the *outside* aspect of reality at all levels.

Therefore matter, and all bodies, including the human body, should be held with a kind of reverence. Remember, in the Vedantic teachings of Hinduism, hidden within matter is life, hidden in life is mind, and hidden in mind is conscious awareness. We could hold matter itself as an unfathomable mystery containing infinite depths. In the Christian lineage, this brings to mind Jesus' image of the leaven hidden within the bread, the treasure buried within the field, or the seed. Each image suggests that there lives hidden within the external dimension a dynamic, living potential for more abundance. That potential is the Wholeness that everything is lived *by* – in other words, G_d.

Science is concerned with physics – the physical realm. But science tends to reduce all of reality to matter. This is a methodological necessity. Science must control for variables and therefore is biased to favour as much simplicity as possible. Which is fine as a methodology, as long as it is named as such. When this methodology becomes an ideology, however, it tends to make assumptions about reality: i.e., that it begins and ends with the physical. But note how different this assumption is from the one discussed above, in which matter, magnificent as it is, is just the exterior dimension of a very dynamic interiority – one which is filled, according to the spiritual vision, with G_d.

For example, consciousness, for most of science, is considered an epiphenomenon, that is, a product of matter. It is assumed that mind and consciousness come out of the grey matter of our brain.

Much of neurology continues to proceed on the assumption that the brain is the cause of mind and consciousness. It is important to realize that this is unproven and in fact this thinking is the result of a belief system, not science. It is metaphysics: metaphysical materialism, to be precise, not science. Thanks to the scientific method we now know that there is a *correlation*, for example, between certain parts of the brain and specific feelings and memories. There is also a correlation between feelings of attachment and love and the release of the hormone oxytocin. But *correlation* should not be confused with *causation*. The brain doesn't cause love, but some of its hormonal functions are correlated with it.

Many quantum physicists are now coming to the conclusion that mind or consciousness is more fundamental than matter, and that matter emerges or crystallizes out of mind. They arrive at this conclusion mostly because when they examine matter at a quantum level it doesn't hold together very well. It turns out that we are mostly space and that this space is not empty or inert. It consists of fields of energy that are dynamic and that exhibit intelligence.

Grounded in metaphysical materialism, science does not concern itself with evolution beyond the biological realm. Yet there is much evidence that evolution does indeed occur in a correlative fashion in the physical, relational, cultural, and social systems domains.

The late New Testament scholar Marcus Borg, bless his soul, taught progressive Christians to take the Bible seriously, but not literally. At this point in our evolution as a species, we could change that adage to "take *science* seriously, but not literally." Modernity, with its focus on empiricism, rightly displaced the authority of church and her priesthood in order to liberate humanity and to free the arts and culture from the narrow perspective of the medieval institution and worldview. But I'm afraid that the modern materialistic worldview is in some ways more myopic than the medieval worldview. Of course, we can be grateful that, thanks to science, we don't use leeches or bleeding to cure diseases. And the advent of the computer and worldwide web surely has untapped potential for good. But trying to explain all of reality in and through physics results in a very narrow scope of view.

A few hundred years ago, it was necessary to appeal to the authority of scripture if your truth claim was to be valid. Today there is an authority ascribed to science that is often unconscious. For example, creationists, who now call their school of thought "intelligent design," recognized that to be taken seriously they would have to ground their beliefs in science. This led to silly claims that the Bible was factually, empirically true in all its details. This was a dramatic and ironic nod by fundamentalist Christians to the power of empiricism and the new priesthood, scientists.

Even progressive Christians get caught up in the authority of the empirical method feeling like they need to ground their spiritual intuition in what can be corroborated by the science of physics, neurology, or biology, or indeed the science of evolution. The end result is that progressive Christianity (for example) can be very dry and rationalistic. We need to be grateful to the scientific method, absolutely, as science is a very powerful tool. But we also need to be alert to the dangers of reductionism.

I've mentioned that an ancient perennial philosophy principle states that the "higher" cannot be *produced* by the "lower," yet it does emerge *through* the lower. By affirming that the potential for life, mind, higher consciousness, and "whatever might be next after higher consciousness" evolutionarily speaking is already enfolded within matter, we can understand the evolutionary process as a sacred unfolding.

As I stated in the first chapter, this doesn't mean that there is a blueprint for evolution. There is novelty, spontaneity, and chance built into the purposive nature of the universe.

Evolution at all levels – physical, cultural, social and spiritual – is driven not merely by physicalistic forces (such as the neo-Darwinian focus on survival), but by a sacred impulse for self-transcendence. This impulse, I am persuaded, is love. As we mentioned, David Loye, in his book *Darwin's Lost Theory of Love*, uses extensive research to note that Darwin has been misinterpreted by the vast majority of scientists, who think that mere survival instinct is the driver of evolution. Darwin himself claimed that, for humans, love is by far the more important driver. For the spiritually inclined, this makes sense of the religious intuition that love is the Source of all that is.

The so-called neo-Darwinian synthesis tends to reduce other drivers of self-transcendence – such as love; service; and the pursuit of beauty, truth, and goodness – to varying expressions of the survival instinct. This kind of reductionism is too often uncritically swallowed by the public because of the authority we ascribe to the dominant scientific paradigm, as though the drivers of evolution do not themselves evolve.

3. Evolution displays purpose

This might not seem controversial to the average person. But believe me, it is. The current scientific climate does not allow for purpose. There are many reasons for this, but the big reason is the fear that any conversation about purpose leads to a traditional God, who engineers the universe according to His will. This is a non-starter for empirical science, for understandable reasons.

However, it needs once again to be stated that the shift from methodological necessity – that is, the need to assume that no external influences are meddling with natural laws – to an ideology that there is no purpose is again metaphysics, not science. The conclusion that the universe, including human life, is little more than a happy accident is both unwarranted and contrary to our fundamental intuition as humans. The modernist and late postmodernist philosophical conclusion that any purpose we may ascribe to our lives is not inherent in the universe, but is rather an arbitrary projection of humans, is itself a belief system – no different than a religious belief system, actually.

To say that the universe is unfolding purposefully does not mean that there is a single purpose, or that a God is directing the evolutionary process toward some predetermined end.

How do I know that the evolutionary process is purposeful? I'll get to that, but first a story. I was once speaking with a colleague at a conference. I got up and talked about the cosmos as displaying purpose. She got up and talked about how the universe was cold and indifferent to our plight and to the plight of Earth. The best we could do was to muster up a little bit of empathy. But we didn't have any wind at our back. This was very curious to me. I knew this woman to be deeply caring and compassionate. She proceeded in life as though she had purpose, as though she had a vocation, in fact, to be an agent of compassion.

The only way that one can draw the conclusion that the universe is cold, indifferent, and purposeless is to extract oneself from the universe itself, and become an objective observer of a process that doesn't include you – as if you are over here, a compassionate person, looking out there at a universe that is cold and indifferent. But the experience of the evolutionary mystic is that there is no separation anywhere in the universe. You *are* the warm-heartedness and that warm-heartedness *is* the ever-evolving universe in the form of you! We are, as we'll see in the next tenet, the universe's most intimate expression. It seems a little absurd to tell an audience that the universe is purposeless and cold, while acting in a purposeful and warm way. This is a schizoid separation born of a case of mistaken identity.

So you, dear reader, are the best evidence that the universe is purposeful. When you feel the longing to love, the desire to make an offering of your life, the willingness to sacrifice on behalf of your children, the desire to master a trade or increase a competency so that your work can be more meaningful, you are acting "on-purpose." We are not generating purpose out of nowhere. The universe comes equipped with purpose. It's standard equipment.

Once we have awakened from the cultural trance of separation consciousness, we feel the direct and immediate urge to participate in the purposeful evolution of the universe. In fact, this consent to consciously evolve in love is, for the mystic orientation, what we showed up for.

4. We are not separate from the evolutionary process, but rather its most intimate expression

Evolution is a theory that one can study, absolutely. But the danger here is that you miss the existential truth that evolution is happening in you, through you, and as you. You are the interior, personal expression of a creative process that is billions of years old. It has awakened in you.

All the creative potential inherent in the great radiance of the Big Bang is coming into being in you. You are the presence of all that creative energy organized into a human form. You are the concentrated amalgam of all the non-organic and organic life forms that have come before you.

When I say that you are evolution's most intimate expression, I mean that in *you*, in all of us, the universe's potential for personhood is in the process of being realized. The creativity out of which a universe emerged is realizing its capacity for free will, agency, higher purpose, conscious self-awareness, love, etc., through you!

As you consent to consciously surrender your life to this spirit-driven evolutionary current to grow, to learn, to open your heart, and to allow your curiosity to break you out of old habits of being, you realize our own creative potential.

5. Our spiritual longings drive the evolutionary process

There is an ancient Talmudic saying: "Every blade grass has an angel whispering in its ear… 'grow, grow, grow.'" This divine imperative emanates from that Mystery and Source religion has called G_d. One of the implications of this tenet is that to feel this evolutionary current alive within yourself, to hear your own angels whispering in your ear "grow, grow, grow," and to follow this allurement, is to feel a direct connection with Source. G_d is as close as our deepest longings.

To listen to and follow the whisper of our holy longings is to allow the originating and ongoing Wholeness or Health (G_d) to live *through* us, and *as* us. As Paul writes in his letter to the Romans, "for we do not know how to pray as we ought, but the Spirit intercedes with sighs too deep for words" (8:26). Our holy longings are the way Spirit prays *us*. In this conscious consent to honouring our holy longings as expressions of Spirit, we experience an increasing sense of living from wholeness in our lives. In evolutionary spirituality, allowing ourselves to be transformed by this Wholeness is the deep meaning of salvation.

It is important to restate that G_d's way of being present in our holy longings is always persuasive and never coercive. We always have choice about whether we consent to organize our lives around our deepest longings, say for love.

The biblical characters of Solomon and Elisha illustrate the transformation that occurs when we allow ourselves to be apprehended by our yearnings. The one yearning that Solomon organized his life around was wisdom. He went on to become a king who was identified with his wise judgments. Elisha's heart burns with only one longing: to be granted a double portion of the spirit of his master, Elijah. This single-mind focus on our deepest yearnings is a form of prayer and evolutionary development.

Our yearnings do not need to be so grand. In fact, I recommend as an exercise doing a time chart of your life. Reflect decade by decade on what your deepest longings were in each decade. In my teens, it was for mastery in sports. In my 20s, it was for meaning. In my third decade, I wanted recognition. In my 40s and 50s I wanted more than anything else to be taken by love. We become what we most yearn for. This is the art and grace of manifestation.

Our longings naturally evolve over time. If I am a man in my 50s still yearning for mastery at a sport, as opposed to simply the pleasure of feeling my body move, I would judge that my ego is frozen in a particular image of myself. This is desire, as distinct from holy longing.

When we are "in" our holy longing, we are "in" G_d. When we consent to follow these longings and to let our lives be shaped by them, we are actively completing or realizing that longing of G_d for our world, for all creation, and for us. The evolutionary mystic becomes one with this holy longing and in so doing unites with G_d.

Holy longing, as distinct from egoic desire, leads to freedom, an expanded sense of self (cosmic self), and an absence of the desperate striving that reflects a self that is not evolving. There is what choreographer Martha Graham called the "blessed unrest," which needs to be distinguished from the unholy striving for more of the same – more wealth, food, sex, alcohol, drugs – which results in all manner of addiction. The blessed unrest arises from the conscious participation in the evolutionary impulse to unite with the being and the becoming of G_d.

The psalmist expresses holy longing as opposed to desire: "Out of the depths I cry to you, O LORD" (Psalm 130:1).

What is your G_d cry? To name this, to enact it, to actually hear our souls crying out to G_d does not require thinking about it. The more you have to think about it, the further you will be from it. This is something you get at by feeling. The feeling rises up and apprehends you. It grabs you by the gonads, and takes over your whole being.

In Genesis 24, the story is told of Abraham sending his chief servant off to a foreign land to get a wife for his son, Isaac. He makes his servant swear, while placing his hand on Abraham's testicles, that he will not bring back a Canaanite wife. The meaning is clear; Abraham's lineage is on the line. This plea is coming from Abraham's very depths.

Our longings are unique to us and evolve over time. But if I was to take a stab at a universal cry (and this extends to the other-than-human realms as well), my candidate would be self-transcendence, through a process of being recreated by love, again and again.

There is the cry for more that arises from a felt sense of insufficiency, for example, if we don't have enough food to eat, enough nurturing, or enough meaning in our lives. Of course, we will cry out for more. This healthy and natural.

But there is a crying out for more that issues from a contracted self once these basic needs have been met that is *not* healthy. We have enough food, but we crave more. We have enough sex, but we want more. We have enough status, but we want more. We have enough money, but we want more. This cry for more is characteristic of all addictions. It is the cry for more that issues from the contracted self, which does not want to evolve. The addiction is in service to stasis – the refusal to move or to be moved *by* life. This is our consumptive self, which is now expressed on a societal level through our "consumer society." It drives our economy, which is why this economic system is bound to collapse, along with our contracted self.

This is *desire*, not *longing*. The only way to break the cycle of desire is to feel the longing that is being concealed by the desire, which is to feel the grief of living without whatever beautifies and resources the soul. The cry for more that is primordial is for more love, more life, more capacity to see the beauty that is before our eyes. This longing drives the evolutionary process itself. It is woven into the fabric of life. Using theological language, it is the Holy Spirit.

One of the core competencies of evolutionary spirituality is the capacity to distinguish between desire and longing. It is a subtle distinction, because neither will ever be fulfilled. Desire is typically for more of what we already have. It is craving. Longing, on the other hand, is for a deepening. "From the *depths* I cry to you, O G_d." Desire creates habits, neurological and behavioural loops that keep us locked into yesterday. Longing opens us up to new neural pathways being laid down, and breaks us out of routine, making room for a new and more intense future. Desire issues in routines and ruts. In the temporary satisfaction of desire, we may feel free, but it lands us back where we started. Longing leads to adventure and to authentic freedom. It requires risk as an orientation in life. Unfulfilled desire leads to increased contraction, anxiety, and isolation. Unfulfilled longing is expansive. In fact, true longing is not meant to be satiated. It causes us to wonder where we are being led. It connects us more deeply to life, to love, and to freedom.

I have had the experience of being simultaneously filled with all the love my heart can handle, of resting in such grace, and at the same time experiencing the longing to go deeper. "Go to the limits of your longing," writes the poet Rainer Maria Rilke. There you will discover that a new horizon of longing opens up to you – requiring only that we die to the limit we have just reached, in order to be born again, drawn by a new limit. And when it comes to love, we are dealing with infinite depth, the very heart of the Divine.

Evolutionary mysticism asks of us, as daily practice, to organize our lives in obedience (to use an old-fashioned metaphor) to our longings. To allow ourselves to feel this cry to G_d is, in the first place, disruptive. It is iconoclastic, shattering all the false idols we have confused with life itself. After the disruption, life reorganizes us around our soul, which is flying, always, always, always to Spirit. Perhaps this is why Jesus is portrayed as saying that a sin against the Holy Spirit is unforgivable (Mark 3:29). The religious authorities were claiming that he was possessed by demonic spirits. But Jesus knew that it was the Holy Spirit animating him. The sin against the Holy Spirit is to allow our desires and addictions to keep us from our holy longings.

There are consequences to chronically resisting our deepest longings (and thereby resisting G_d). Contemporary mystic Thomas Hübl uses the image of being in a fast-flowing river that is sweeping us along. If we can let go and relax into the current, we will be carried. However, if because of fear we cling to the sides of the river, the pull of current will feel even more strong and we will need to hold on tighter. The longer we hold on, the more stress we create. Ultimately, we will become soul sick. And this will manifest in physical symptoms. Our soul wants to release its grip and be swept along by the current. In this letting go, we gain union with G_d by entering into the flow of the evolutionary impulse.

6. Evolution is the unfolding of Love at all levels and scales of reality: matter, life, consciousness, and culture

The premise of this tenet is that G_d is love and that a world made in the image of love emerged from G_d. The evolving world is the divine heart overflowing and being poured out in this dimension of space and time. As we've seen, all reality participates in and is participated by a primordial attraction and communion dynamic. This is the attraction of atoms, molecules, cells; the attraction of the sun and Earth through gravity; and, in the human realm, we call this attraction and desire to be in communion with All That Is, "love." This is what motivates all mystics – this deep yearning to realize our fundamental connectedness and unity with All That Is.

Paul writes in 1 Corinthians 13 about what love is and is not. You could summarize that section on love by saying that love is never coercive. It never uses force. It is patient, kind, and gentle. This means that the presence of G_d in the evolutionary trajectory of the universe is always persuasive.

Think about the way love works in a family. The best that parents can do is to create a milieu of love, where the children know that they are cared for, fed, attuned to, resourced, and sent on their way. The parent who tries to engineer or control their child's future will soon find out that it's not possible. Parents who engineer their children's lives rob them of sovereignty and dignity. Teilhard de Chardin uses the image of a divine milieu of love to point to the way. The best that parents can do is to create a milieu of love. G_d's love pervades the universe in a non-coercive manner.

We are lived by this immense creative impulse. This tenet makes the claim that that current is the flow of love. Love is the "divine milieu" in which this continually evolving miracle of life is unfolding. Humans are the creatures in whom the evolutionary capacity of being aware of this milieu emerged.

Our vocation, using the image of the river current, is to release into this current of love and not cling to the riverbank – which is our ego and the many faces of fear. The evolutionary mystic realizes that when she is living in right relationship to reality and releasing into this current of love, she is being carried *by* love.

7. We are the creativity of the universe in human form

Cosmologist Brian Swimme notes that humans are reconfigured expressions of the Big Bang in human form. We are what the Big Bang looks like after billions of years of evolution – all that creativity manifested *in* and *as* us. In fact, we are the creative impulse in the form of a human being. And that creativity wants to bring forth new worlds *through* us. It is our responsibility to steward that creativity by removing obstacles, within and without, that stifle our creativity.

This is why we feel most alive when we are creative, when we are having a new thought, seeing a new perspective, wearing a new look, embarking on a new venture or adventure, or developing a new program. When we participate in the emergence of a new thing, we are participating in the same creativity that brought forth a universe. Theologically, we are expressing our Christ nature when we are creative.

It's important to understand that it's not just artists who are creative. We actively create our own experience in every moment. Our own lives are the most essentially creative act we will ever engage in. We select from the thousands of sensations that bombard our nervous system through our five senses only a small sliver, and from this selection fashion our reality. We interpret this sliver of experience by filtering it through our worldview, beliefs, values, and emotional trauma. We don't see the world as it is, we see it as *we are*.

In my experience of engaging in an ancient Amazonian sacred ceremony that involves consuming *Ayahuasca* (a plant-based hallicogenic or entheogenic extract that has been used for thousands of years by indigenous peoples) these filters are removed and we get a glimpse into dimensions of reality that were always present, but which we chose not perceive. Much that I had filtered out of my experience, necessarily (in order to function) was temporarily suspended. Even this filtering out of the unseen dimensions of reality in order to gain a localized self-sense is itself a creative act.

The more conscious we are of how and when we are doing this the more we grow in our capacity to consciously create the future. Conscious awareness also allows us increasingly, with training, to see the world as it truly is, and to know it on its own terms. This constitutes conscious evolution and is the life of the evolutionary mystic, who takes responsibility for bringing to consciousness the various filters that define his or her experience. In so doing, he or she opens up to new perspectives, and a new power to shape a future that is not wholly determined by the past.

Usually, we create our reality through filters that keep us locked in the past – what Eastern traditions call karma. We all have the experience of re-enacting our childhood trauma, or choosing the wrong partner over and over again. Actually, there is no wrong choice. We choose exactly those aspects of reality to focus on, and those persons, that will provoke our evolution.

As we learn those lessons, by seeing our life experience as wisdom teacher, we learn the competency of bringing our filtering systems to consciousness. As we do, we evolve our capacity to bring forth a future that is not solely the product of the past. We grow in freedom, in other words. It is the freedom to be *determiners* of the future and not merely *determined* by the past.

For example, if we use the modernist worldview as a lens for filtering reality, we will bring forth a world that is very different from a medieval worldview. The world will be less mysterious. We will validate reality through what can be empirically proven. We will elevate reason above passion and intuition.

We will be suspicious, if not disdainful, of religion. None of these things are wrong in and of themselves. But there is a lot of reality that is excluded by using this filter.

If we were physically or emotionally abused as children, we may form an unconscious belief that we are bad. This belief will act as a filter for our experience, and we will find ways to validate this belief, by creating our lives in such a way that proves our badness. We may enter therapy and discover all the ways that this belief is hampering our future, keeping us on the wheel of karma, and creating all kinds of suffering.

The ultimate goal may be to consciously suspend our filtering systems, to accept reality as it actually comes to us without overly imposing meanings and interpretations. Through meditation, for example, we can learn to temporarily suspend all thoughts about reality. We can experience reality as one continuous flow of creativity and know ourselves to be one organizing centre of consciousness that is being lived by a Mind and Heart that is living in and through all of reality.

It is commonplace in liberal Christianity to refer to ourselves as co-creators. It is true, but in my experience the reason that this is true is never explained. It is merely asserted, and the necessary skills and roadmaps for how to realize this identity are rarely taught.

8. We are the personalization of the universe. Human-making is the end goal of evolution in the human realm

It has taken 13.8 billion years of evolution to arrive at personhood in the human being. Personhood includes free will, the capacity for moral responsibility, agency (to co-create new futures), conscious self-awareness, and love (the capacity to consistently offer one's life in the service of another person, or a higher purpose). While humans may well be serving as the foundation for the emergence of some higher form of life, the present task for us is to live into or fully realize our personhood (humanity).

It has been said by many that humans are *made*, not *born*. For over 100 years, paleontologists have been looking for the "missing link," the primate that bridged the gap between the ape and the human. But in his book *Biblical Faith: An Evolutionary Approach*, theologian Gerd Theissen asks us to consider the possibility that *we* are that missing link. In other words, we are still very much in the process of becoming human. (More will be said about this in Chapter Six.)

Earlier cultures assumed that children would need to be initiated into their humanity. Adolescents went through grueling tests before they would be recognized as adults. Other tribes used vision quests, which again were rigorous rituals of initiation. Today, cosmologist Brian Swimme points out that the average child is initiated into what it means to be human by the media advertisements of big corporations.

Conscious evolution describes the process by which we embrace this sacred vocation of becoming human. It means that we trust our deepest, most holy longings and actively participate in the removal of any physical, emotional, psychological, or spiritual obstacles standing in the way of their realization. This describes a core practice of evolutionary mysticism.

Given that personhood is the highest achievement of the evolutionary process that we know about, I conclude that G_d (the Originating Love and Wisdom out of which a world emerged and continues to emerge) cannot be less than personal, but is infinitely more. This doesn't mean that G_d is "a" person. But that G_d is whatever we mean by personal *plus*. And *that* is the image that we are realizing when we are consciously evolving. We are, in other words, "godding" to the extent that we are actively removing all obstacles that are impeding this sacred vocation from being realized.

The early church saw in the man Jesus of Nazareth one who had realized personhood. It concluded that this is what G_d, the Wholeness that is the source of All That Is, would look like and act like in the form of a human being. We will see in Chapter Six that Jesus seems to have identified with Ezekiel's image of the Son of Man, or the Child of the Human One. To realize our humanity is to realize our divine nature.

This human-making requires letting go of all that is not human or what the spiritual lineage has called purgative practices.

Jesus himself was "driven" into the wilderness precisely to bring to consciousness and gain the capacity to manage, the earliest instincts that we share with our animal lineage. He was "tempted" by security, status, and sustenance," three of the four early evolutionary drivers for sure. (Sexual desire would be the fourth). We could call them instincts of the survivor self. But these are precisely what he went into the wilderness to gain freedom from. By bringing them to consciousness and choosing to be motivated by higher spiritual impulses, he redeemed these earlier instincts – by which I mean he helped to locate these earlier instincts within an ultimate context of love. He evolved into the prototype of what it means to be human.

——— FIVE ———

Unconventional Images of Jesus

The present meaning of the historical Jesus
has been the unconscious agenda of the Jesus-quest for these past two centuries.
Driving that enormous undertaking was an inchoate desire among Christian scholars
to recover something numinous and lost within themselves,
and within contemporary religion.

— Walter Wink

Jesus as evolutionary provocateur

There is little question that we create Jesus in our own image. We inevitably project on to him what we regard as most important and critical to the human condition and then interpret his teaching through these filters. All us are embedded within worldviews that define for us what matters most and how we interpret reality. Scholars have been trying to come up with a definitive portrait of Jesus for centuries. The so-called "quest for the historical Jesus" has occupied academia for the past 100 years. Divine saviour; second person of the Trinity; mystic; social prophet; magician; healer; Jewish peasant-rabbi: these are just a sampling of the images humanity has laid over Jesus.

New Testament scholar Walter Wink is right when he says, "Our picture of Jesus reflects not only Jesus, but the person portraying Jesus."[1] Those interested in discovering the historical Jesus are in truth animated in this search by a primordial desire to know our own humanity. We are allured

---

1 Ibid., 10.

by the attraction of an archetypal "human" that is calling us to realize our deepest potentials.

Wink proposes that this search for the historical Jesus is in truth the search for the true human, or the archetypal human. The various critical tools that scholars have utilized to "get to" the "real" Jesus are important, in that they help us to discover the true human *in* and *through* the portraits of the man Jesus of Nazareth given to us in the gospel accounts.

"In short, the quest for the historical Jesus has all along been the quest for the human Jesus. There is no need for consensus or unanimity on what constitutes an authentic Jesus tradition,"[2] Wink writes. Nevertheless, these constructions must be supported by the text if they are to be credible.

In this spirit, I'd like to add a few more images to the mix, beginning with *evolutionary provocateur*. Whatever else can be said about Jesus, it is clear that he intended to evolve his own Jewish lineage. He was motivated, not to abolish his tradition, but to help it *evolve*. Many of his teachings began with "you have heard it said, but I say unto you...," indicating that he had new wisdom to offer, wisdom that would transcend, but include, the tradition. His teaching that you cannot put new wine into old wine skins, or use unshrunk cloth to mend an old garment, without destroying the new wine or the old garment, indicates his evolutionary intentions. Rather, one needs a new wineskin and a new garment – that is, a new mind and a new heart to even be able to hear the new wisdom that he is teaching. Through parables, teachings, and healing, he provoked the new mind and heart – one that I am calling *evolutionary mysticism*.

What precisely was it, is it, that Jesus provokes? The future. As I've already stated, I don't mean the future as tomorrow or ten years down the road. I mean the future as the highest possibility available now. Quite simply, Jesus confronted every single person he met with a vision of their future as the highest possibility available to them. That is, individuals saw in him and through him another possible future for themselves, a future in which their humanity was

---

2 John Dominic Crossan, *The Essential Jesus: Original Sayings and Earliest Images* (Eugene, OR: Wipf and Stock, 2008), 8.

deepened, liberated, and more aligned with their essential nature. In Jesus, they were confronted by a more evolved human being, whose vocation was to help *others* to evolve. To encounter him was to activate a depth dimension that is hidden beneath the surface personality – the true human expressing itself through us.

"Take up your mat and walk."

"Your faith has made you well."

"Do you want to be healed?"

"Go and sin no more."

"Sell all that you have and give it to the poor."

With injunctions such as these, Jesus conveyed to those he healed that a new future was possible.

To the rich, young ruler who comes asking how he might find eternal life, Jesus instructs to keep the commandments. The young man has already done this faithfully. But he must go beyond the ethic of obedience if he wants to evolve. Jesus perceives that this young ruler has been possessed by wealth. To realize his future today, in the present, Jesus invites him to loosen his grip and follow him. But the man is not ready to take this evolutionary step and walks away (Matthew 19:16–22).

On the other hand, Zacchaeus, the tax collector, claims his future. Jesus invites himself over to dinner, even though Zacchaeus was technically, a "sinner." Zacchaeus then gives away half his possessions to the poor, and offers to pay back anybody he has defrauded four times the amount (Luke 19:1-10).

Jesus was proclaiming the end of one era for humanity and the dawning of a new one – one person at a time. His teaching was apocalyptic in one sense, but not in the way most people associate with that word. He wasn't proclaiming a literal end to the world, but rather the end of *my* world and *your* world as we have come to know it. That world, which shut down the future (whether by external authorities or inner belief systems) is, or could be over. The choice is ours. That said, if we do *not* choose our highest possibility as a species and as individuals, the consequences could be truly apocalyptic.

Jesus' very being was a proclamation of what the new human looked like.

His spiritual freedom, his wholeness, his power, his compassion, his wisdom was now available to all humans. In his teachings, he conveyed new spiritual wisdom, which, if adhered to, effectively overturned the world of conventional wisdom. It represented nothing less than the emergence of a new way of seeing, a new worldview. New Testament scholar Dominic Crossan gave this a fancy name: sapiential (wisdom) eschatology (end times).[3] Upon hearing and integrating this new wisdom, one way of being human ends and another way begins. The future, as the highest unrealized possibility, emerges today.

As provocateur of a new way, Jesus brought into view and within reach one's highest possibility for being human. Moral righteousness and an ethic of obedience would be included but transcended by the living, interiorly felt, wisdom of love. Living superficially by adhering to external rules and codes of conduct would give way to living by participating in, and being participated *by*, a hidden depth dimension, which is the Source of life itself. Self-limiting beliefs, and social and cultural barriers were removed.

Idolatry, the attribution of life and allegiance to that which is in truth dead, is transcended through repentance (turning from death to life) and then by entering the Kin(g)dom – that , living through the new wisdom. (More will be said about idolatry and the kin(g)dom of God below.)

This is what makes Jesus' so-called "hard sayings" hard. Most listeners and readers, then and now, try to understand his teachings with the mind of the old human, operating from conventional wisdom and morality. But as we've seen, to understand Jesus we need to undergo a *metanoia*, which means literally receiving a higher mind.

Jesus' teachings evoked what I call the OOPS! (Old Operating System) phenomenon. People would hear him through an old operating system that had worked well in its day. But Jesus' wisdom replaced that operating system with an upgraded one that changed everything. He was so misunderstood, then and now, because we haven't updated our operating system.

For example, in his parable about the labourers in the vineyard, the mo-

---

3 John Dominic Crossan, *The Essential Jesus: Original Sayings and Earliest Images* (Eugene, OR: Wipf and Stock, 2008), 8.

rality of fairness is transcended by a higher moral principle of grace that is born of love. In the story, day labourers gather in the morning hoping that someone will show up, negotiate a day's wages, and employ them. One employer hires men for the full day, for a half-day, and then finally he hires some men for just one hour at the end of the working day. With each man he negotiates a fair wage. But with those he hired at the end of the day, he was very generous, paying them the same as what he paid the other two groups of men.

This parable offends even modern day sensibilities. Every time I preached on this text, I would need to contend with those who thought it was unfair. Jesus consciously replaces one good (a fair and equal wage) with a higher good (abundant generosity). OOPS! The good becomes the enemy of the better.

The employer reminds the resentful labourers, who worked longer hours, that he had openly negotiated with them their wage. He then adds, "Do you begrudge my generosity?"

Which gets right to the point. Jesus was provoking good, religious people, who had strived diligently to be such for decades, and their ancestors too, who had tried to live the good life for generations. Then Jesus announced that G_d's grace extends to Gentiles as well, not just "our" group. Even though these Johnny-come-lately Gentiles (the labourers chosen at the end of the day who nevertheless received the same wage as those hired at the beginning) lived unrighteous lives according to the moral codes of the Jews, they were being offered the same grace. Love, grace, and generosity trump conventional ideas of fairness and adherence to strict moral codes; and conventional notions of who is in and who is out based on ethnicity, religious practices, and beliefs. The teaching does not abolish moral codes, fair labour practice, Jewish identity, or sacred rituals. Rather, it contextualizes them, setting them within the higher wisdom of love.

The same theme is played out in the parable of the prodigal son. The youngest son takes his inheritance, squanders it, and ends up working for Gentiles on a pig farm (the height of indignity for a Jew). Then the son "comes to his senses." He returns home and his father welcomes him with open arms. But in the wings, the elder brother, who chose to stay home and be the "faithful, good son" seethes in resentment. Again, the love of the father trumps strict moral codes. Again, *one* good (dedication and loyalty) is contextualized by a *higher* good (the love of the father, and the desire of the younger son for adventure, and to gain direct experience).

OOPS! The elder son is functioning from a worldview that values above all loyalty and adherence to tradition. He sees his father operating according to a value that transcends, but includes loyalty – love – and he is either forced to repent and use a new operating system, or stay bitter and resentful.

Jesus did the same with the purity and dietary codes of his own religion. He maintained that it's not what goes into a person (clean, washed, kosher), but what comes out of them (words and deeds) that determines a person's holiness (Matthew 15:11). What goes in, he says, goes through the digestive system and is eliminated into the sewer. What comes out (words and actions) persists as a potentially positive or negative influence. That is what matters! OOPS. For those who had identified their spirituality with dietary codes (and thus turned this practice into idolatry) this was not good news. Either repent and upgrade your system, or be threatened by the new wisdom.

Jesus was accused of being a drunkard and a sinner because many of the people he chose to eat with – women, poor, socially ostracized, as well as wealthy collaborators with Rome (tax-collectors) – were considered unclean. This made him unclean and impure by association. Jesus acted as evolutionary provocateur exposing the idolatry of his own religion and creating space for it to open up.

It should go without saying that every religion, including the one started in Jesus' name, is susceptible to idolatry. The irony is profound that the majority of Christians – who adhere to a strict interpretation of his teaching and a shallow moralism – made Jesus himself into an idol, as opposed to drawing from the living wisdom that animated him and that is also within them.

Many of Jesus' healings were not merely physical healings; they were also social in nature. These healings were his way of reincorporating the socially ostracized – a woman with a flow of blood, a prostitute, lepers, the blind, Gentiles, the very poor – back into the fold. Jesus was enacting a principle of the radical inclusivity of G_d's love. When the rules, codes, and all the religious regulations excluded the most vulnerable, Jesus tapped into a wisdom that informed him that all these rules were made to serve humans. When humans started serving them instead, the rules became false gods that needed to be exposed as unreal and superficial.

When we live by these external codes, we effectively offload our responsibility for knowing *from within* what is right and wrong, and what is required in this moment. The codes become idols that we slavishly obey (or we suffer punishment from God). But the spontaneous, inner wisdom that Jesus wanted his followers to access and live by is fluid, spontaneous, and somewhat wild – wild in the sense that it operates outside of consensus reality. You never really know what love will demand in the moment.

For example, on one occasion when Jesus gathered with the disciples, it had become clear that he was in grave trouble. The Roman authorities were after him and his intuition told him that he would be executed. A woman named Mary, displaying great intuition and compassion, approached and anointed his feet with very expensive oil. Taking him at his word, she was effectively starting the preparation of his body for death. Judas, who would ultimately betray Jesus, was more of an ideologue than a mystic. He complained to Jesus that the oil could have been sold and the money gained distributed to the poor. But Jesus, functioning from a transrational (which includes but transcends rationality) moral wisdom, told him to lay off. On this occasion Mary's gesture of compassion was exactly what was needed. Furthermore, Jesus said, "the poor will be with you always" (John 12:2-8). OOPS!

This is another of those "hard sayings" that drives postmodern, sensitive types crazy. But love trumps ideology in the sacred wisdom that was operating within Jesus. In this moment, under these circumstances, the woman did exactly the right thing. Jesus' image of G_d included, of course, a heart for justice. But it wasn't a hardened, ideological position. Her gesture of compassion *was* the justice being called for.

Another example of how Jesus privileged spontaneous gestures even when they undermined consensus reality (or *especially when* they did so), is the story of Mary and Martha (Luke 10:38–42). On his way to Jerusalem, Jesus would stay at his friend Lazarus' place in Bethany, just on the outskirts of the city. On this occasion, Jesus was teaching. Mary was supposed to be making lunch. But Mary took off her apron, stopped preparing the food, and refused to act like most women in first-century Mediterranean cultures. She decided to "sit at the feet of Jesus." In other words, she decided to exit the patriarchal box that women were put in and become a *student* of Jesus. Martha pitches Jesus to put Mary in her place. But Jesus replies, "Mary has chosen the better part." It's difficult to convey how radical this was. It undermined patriarchy's role for women. And it also sent a message that women were equal to men in the Jesus movement. Again, this couldn't have happened if Jesus' image of G_d was conventional or traditional.

Jesus consistently pushed the boundaries of his lineage, and of the lives of individuals, as an evolutionary provocateur.

This story continues to offend good church people, especially those who like Martha choose to serve by staying in the kitchen. Others in the congregation come to their defense. Of course, these good souls should be recognized and celebrated for their contribution to the community. But the parable actually addresses Martha's *resentment* of Mary. If Martha truly had been content to stay in the kitchen and serve the desserts at the potluck, she wouldn't have been so upset. The parable is for the Marthas of the world who are feeling suffocated by their designated roles. And yet they lack Mary's courage to break out of the box. OOPS!

Mary repented and entered the kin(g)dom of G_d. Martha wasn't ready. The first stage of Martha's liberation is to understand that her own resentment is a signal to her that it is time to evolve. Jesus was acting as evolutionary provocateur for a patriarchal culture that stifled the freedom of women. Mary broke out of her assigned role in choosing to sit at the rabbi's feet.

What this means is perhaps obvious, but needs to be stated: to be in the lineage of Jesus does not mean turning his teachings into new laws, new ideology, or new rules for life. Jesus was about exposing this kind of idolatry. To be in the world in the spirit of Jesus is to be iconoclastic. It is to break open false idols, predetermined positions, and politically-correct thinking so that we can discover the *true* life that is animating our lives. It is to exhibit spontaneity, novelty, and a subversive wisdom in a way that does not tow the party line – even if that party line is "progressive." It is to refuse to be pigeonholed or to pigeonhole oneself for the sake of comfort and certainty.

One of the ways that Jesus filled the role of evolutionary provocateur was to present images and stories that required listeners to expand their own image of G_d. He provoked, in other words, new space for G_d to be G_d.

As the Sufi poet Rumi wrote,

God comes to you in whatever image you have been able to form of God.

The wiser and broader and more gorgeous the image,

the more the grace and power can flow from the throne into your heart.

God is saying, I am where my servant thinks of me.

Whatever image my servant forms of me, there I will be.

I am the servant of my servant's image of me.

Be careful then my servants

and purify, attune, and expand your thoughts about me

for they are My house.[4]

The other reason, of course, to be careful with our images of G_d is that those images, being the highest and noblest we can imagine, are what we ourselves aspire to. As much as anything else, Jesus was provoking those who encountered him to look at their own image of G_d, and to determine whether it was "gorgeous" enough, or spacious enough, to allow for grace and love to overflow, *and* for *them* to grow *into*.

For example, it's very challenging for any of us to free ourselves from an image of G_d as judge and rule-maker. This is because the voice of withering self-judgment emanates from within our own minds, a legacy of cultural and family trauma. We impose rules and regulations on ourselves so that we don't have to risk unleashing that inner voice, which would land us in a state of shame. Traditional expressions of religion simply project this inner voice onto

4 Andrew Harvey, trans. *Light upon Light: Inspirations from Rumi* (New York: Jeremy P. Tarcher/Penguin, 1996), 131.

G_d and, if we hear it from a pulpit, it resonates deeply with our own unredeemed inner critic.

Jesus as lover

The image implicit in John's story of Jesus and the wedding feast in Cana is of G_d as lover and as celebrant of love. This G_d, known in Jesus, places the highest value on celebrating love (John 2:1–11). John uses this story as the first "sign" of Jesus' glory.

I don't know what narrow Christian moralists make of this story of Jesus turning water into wine. I mean, it's a lot of wine – approximately 500 litres. Of the good stuff. Jesus keeps the love flowing.

With Jesus, love is front and centre. Love has drawn the couple together, and the couple's love has drawn the whole village together. This allurement of love describes, in evolutionary mysticism, the fundamental evolutionary driver of the universe. (We've seen how Charles Darwin himself believed this.)

Jesus would have known Isaiah's imagery of the wedding between G_d and G_d's people and the land (Isaiah 62:4). He was drawing on this higher and broader image of G_d from within his own tradition. Both the land and the people would be redeemed by intimate union with G_d. Israel's name was "Forsaken," the land's name was "Desolate." But their destiny would be transformed by this marriage to the "builder of Israel." The land's name would then be "Married." Israel's name would no longer be Desolate, but "My Delight Is In You."

I've presided at close to 1,000 weddings in my 28 years of ministry. I confess to becoming jaded over the years knowing that half of these marriages would end in divorce, including two of my own. But there was always a moment in every marriage when the ideal and the promise of the ceremony softened my heart. You could see (not in all, but in the vast majority) that these couples believed that, with each other, they could accomplish anything. Their delight was in each other. Their hearts were opened and each was more whole with the other than they were on their own. The promise of an abiding love is what animated them.

The promise of such love points, in my opinion and experience, to Reality.

We taste its sweetness when we fall in love. When *I* fell in love, I remember a couple of friends assuring me that this phase wouldn't last. It was a biochemical trick of nature to ensure the perpetuation of our species. But it is the height of cynicism to reduce love to physics and biology. We've seen that it wasn't Darwin himself who did this, but rather the zealots of scientific materialism. If we are willing to do the necessary psychological, emotional, and spiritual work of discovering how we have closed our hearts to love, and if we have come to a place in our life where nothing else matters quite so much, love keeps deepening long after the wedding is over. The wine never runs out, because the wine is love and this is what drives the forward momentum of the cosmos.

This is the point of this first miracle in John's gospel. Five hundred litres of wine is kind of like saying that if you invite Jesus to the party, the wine (of love) never actually runs out. It just keeps getting better and better. The wine that came last in the story is the best vintage, to the amazement of the host and everybody else I'm sure. The best is being saved for the last. This is what happens when two people or a community or a nation set their hearts and minds on consciously evolving the intelligence of love. Or better, allows the love that is Reality to live them.

Cosmologist Brian Swimme talks about the sun and Earth falling in love. Physics calls this primordial attraction gravity. But at the human level it functions as love. A deep attraction forms between sun and Earth which took millions of years to deepen sufficiently for the soul of Earth to awaken in the presence of the sun's light and heat. When it did, all the life that was present as potential, came flowering forth, and, after five billion years of evolution, a species emerged that was able to consciously replicate the cosmic expression of love – heat and light – that brought our planet to life. This is the power of love.

> Someday, after mastering the winds, the waves, the tides and gravity, we shall harness for God the energies of love, and then, for a second time in the history of the world, man will have discovered fire.
>
> – Teilhard de Chardin

In the presence of a human like Jesus of Nazareth, we feel the same kind of allurement as Earth felt in relation to the sun. If we are courageous enough, if we aren't so attached to life as we've known it, if we are willing to risk everything, to die to everything, then we will follow this allurement. And in our following we will find our soul's purpose. We will find what we came for.

I believe that the conditions were right for those first disciples. Jesus knew it. His power of intuition helped to identify those who were ready to leave everything behind in order to follow the allurement of love. Nothing is more powerful or more meaningful. In truth, when we allow ourselves to be taken by love, we align ourselves with the force that allures the whole evolutionary adventure toward fulfillment or completion. What could be more powerful than the force that drives the whole evolutionary process?

Teilhard de Chardin called this absolute power of allurement the Omega Point. He hypothesized that the Christ is the animating power that is drawing all creation toward the realization or perfection (completion) of love initiated by Jesus, and by all souls from every spiritual lineage who are surrendered to love.

When we decide, in the words of my friend Miriam Martineau, to "make love bigger" – bigger than the anger, jealousy, envy, power plays, fear, and despair that we encounter within and without on a daily basis – love grows. When we do the work of bringing our shadow trauma and unconscious life contracts to the light of consciousness, love grows. It "just" requires that we love *Love* more than anything else. This surely is the "glory" that Jesus emanated, confirming for the early community – and for anyone today who still chooses to walk his path and invoke his spirit – that G_d is love.

Jesus as nomad of the new covenant

Sometimes I think it was the fact that Jesus was so unpredictable that got him executed. He didn't follow rules. He responded authentically and freshly to each new experience and challenge. He was an enigma to the religious authorities. Nobody could figure him out, especially his followers. He broke all the rules – healing on the Sabbath, not observing dietary laws, making himself impure by associating with the impure.

Yet he did everything in and from compassion, which meant the religious authorities had no power over him. Rome needed to trump up charges against him. He clearly wasn't a bandit. He wasn't organizing an insurrection, because he advocated non-violence. But he also wasn't afraid of them. The Roman's threat of execution held no sway with him.

Jesus was animated by such creativity that his disciples consistently misinterpreted him. Even in the gospels they are portrayed as not getting his "crazy wisdom."

And we must be honest. There are many editorial additions in the New Testament to Jesus' authentic teachings that are more reflective of the survivalist concerns of an editor, and of the budding institution of the church, than of the evolutionary spirit of Jesus of Nazareth. At times, the editors of the New Testament soften Jesus' teachings to support their more conservative viewpoint. And of course, for at least 1,700 years, after Constantine made Christianity the official religion of the Empire, Christianity was identified with the state and was used as a tool of the state. The evolutionary spirit of Jesus got frozen. And it still is frozen to a degree that is not widely recognized.

Jesus couldn't be pinned down because his image of G_d refused to be pinned down. Jesus' image of G_d, which as we've seen shapes who we are becoming, was more nomadic than institutional.

Nathan, the prophet, had second thoughts about giving the green light to King David's idea of building a temple. G_d says, "I have not lived in a house since the day I brought up the people of Israel from Egypt to this day, but I have been moving about in a tent and a tabernacle…did I ever speak a word with any of the tribal leaders of Israel…saying 'why have you not built me a house of cedar?'" (2 Samuel 7:6–7).

The image of a nomadic G_d fits well with an evolutionary perspective. G_d accompanies the universe on this journey, creating space and time as it all unfolds. This is a G_d who is involved in the historical *becoming* of the people. G_d is in the process, symbolized by G_d moving about in a tent and a tabernacle. A permanent temple is the first stage of divine petrification, of nailing G_d down to the ground – *this* geographical location, *this* perspective and only this perspective, *these* beliefs and *only* these beliefs, *these* rules and *only* these rules. A nomadic, evolving G_d suggests an indeterminate future as well. Who knows where the winds of the journey will blow the whole procession? The G_d of the tent is on an adventure. The G_d of the temple is going nowhere. The priests will make sure of that.

So what we may have here in this passage is G_d fighting for G_d's freedom, requiring that the priesthood be a little more nimble, a little more alert to the promptings of Spirit, and a lot more ready to go when G_d says it's time to pull up stakes.

There are some lessons for the church here, obviously. To take the example of the church I served for almost 30 years, the United Church of Canada has not just *one* temple to contend with, but 1,000s. Many of those temples are falling down. Many have mortgages that prevent communities from doing much of anything, except fundraising. Many have ruinous heating bills, because of inefficient heating plants that are shameful contributors to global warming. Others are filled with uncomfortable pews, which some members considered to be a divinely ordained form of seating. Within a decade or so, if current membership trends continue, the aging progressive church will be moribund. Maybe G_d has already moved on.

The good news is that there are already more nomadic, creative alternatives springing up. The so-called "new monastic movement" is finding spaces to rent in industrial areas of cities. The central mark of this movement is "*relocation* to the abandoned places of empire." My friends, Trevor Malkinson and Rhian Walker, in fact, are close to launching their own expression of this kind of church in Vancouver, Canada. And I need to acknowledge the national office of the United Church of Canada, which is offering financial support to new ministries like this one.

I think the kicker in the 2 Samuel passage comes at the end, when Nathan, speaking for God, says to David, "Dude, I didn't ask you to build me a house, and we did just fine moving around in a tent. But I tell you what. I'll build *you* a house, if you're stuck on having a house."

We so easily and egotistically assume that our vocation is to do stuff *for* G_d, which is kind of laughable. The truth, of course, is that more often than not, under all our posturing, we are doing most of it for ourselves. It's so easy to forget that we are on the receiving end, that we are being lived by this Wholeness that religion calls G_d. Our job is to feel it, to respond to it, and to move, move, move when the Spirit says move.

When the spiritual impulse to become settles down and starts to show signs of wanting the benefits and privileges of the surrounding culture, it becomes religion. Mystery is entombed by certainty. Discernment of Spirit's promptings is replaced by a lifetime vocation – the office of the priest or minister. Trust in Spirit subtly but inexorably gives way to the promise of a pension. Belief substitutes for direct experience. Churches become gatherings of individuals who expect the church to serve their needs. Preservation of buildings consumes more and more of the annual budget. A nomadic, evolving spirituality cannot be pinned down. It cannot be frozen in time. There can be no final iteration of it that can be written in stone.

As Jesus put it, "Nobody who puts his hand to the plough and looks back is fit for the kin(g)dom of G_d" (Luke 9:62). There is a future orientation that includes the tradition, yes. But in the evolutionary spirit of Jesus, it is always breaking new ground, looking for and enacting the new thing G_d is dong. This looking back that Jesus warns against includes looking back at the historical Jesus as the source of our life. Asking "What would Jesus do?" is looking back. Rather, we have an inner compass and a community with whom to discern the promptings of Spirit in the present. The inner compass and source is the living Christ, the Wisdom of G_d, which was also animating Jesus.

A nomadic spirituality is ever-evolving. It's always in the process of becoming, because a nomadic G_d is a creative G_d. "I am about to do a new thing; now it springs forth, do you not perceive it? I will make a way in the wilderness and rivers in the desert" (Isaiah 43:19). This G_d is always "making a way." When we are aligned with this divine creativity, we participate, not in reiteration or repetition, but in "making a way" that is new and often unexpected.

This, not the domesticated version of church that we see throughout the world, reflects the evolutionary spirit of Jesus. Like his G_d, Jesus was continually on the move. This was true in terms of Jesus' strategy of travelling about as an itinerant preacher, teacher, and healer. He had no place to call home, except the heart of his "Father." Dominic Crossan reminds us that, historically, if a small village in Jesus' day had a local healer, it was common practice to build a local industry around him, which would draw pilgrims and their money to the village. But Jesus refused to stay put: "Foxes have holes, and the birds of the air have nests; but the son of man has nowhere to lay his head" (Luke 9:52).

This nomadic storyteller and mystic did not rest in "yesterday's will of G_d."[5] His was a moment-by-moment discernment and enactment of what was true and right. An evolutionary mystic *enjoys* this nomadic orientation, never content to settle for somebody else's truth, or religion's dogmas, or the state's political spin. We suffer this condition of having no place to rest our head.

As noted earlier, the choreography Martha Graham called it "blessed unrest" and "divine dissatisfaction." In this context, I understand blessed unrest to be the condition of those who embrace evolutionary mysticism, the required perspective in this new moment; we are always alert for the new thing, for the future that wants to emerge through us. And we feel from within that as we do so, we are in G_d and G_d is in us.

I wrote a poem inspired by the image of Jesus as nomadic.

Who Told You I Needed A House?
"Who told you I need a house," asks the nomad G_d,
of those who grew weary of the eternal restlessness
thinking S/He might appreciate
a fixed cosmic address,
like a queen or a priest?

---

5 Wink, *Unmasking the Powers: Invisible Forces that Determine Human Existence* (Minneapolis: Fortress Press, 1986), 18.

"Your temples
conceal streams of grace
where once desert pilgrims
found respite, quenched thirst, offered thanks,
and then felt the mistrals moving them on.

"Manager priests in fixed and fancy offices
no longer feel the wind
or hear the gurgling below the foundations.
Carefully ordered liturgies,
closed windows and doors,
ensure that Spirit cannot breathe,
or slip in under the curtains,
and brush the sedentary worshippers
with the longing to move on.

"Am I being too harsh?

"Look into your own eyes.
A creation story explodes when,
in every astonished moment,
you behold
the adventure of life
as my advent.
Look again. Steady.
I am in that retinal explosion –
in the still, black, center,
and in the lines of light that converge
in the you of this moment,
and from the you of this moment
outward to encompass a future
that is born of my restlessness.
Bang!

"If you must build your houses,
then make them sacraments of Sophia –
'more mobile than motion.'

"Tilt the foundation
toward the future,
so that in short order
gravity draws even the most
reluctant inhabitants
out the open door,
to join the procession of pilgrims,
led by the one who has no place
to rest his head.

"Yes, I am unrelenting.
But you knew this.
Your bright and searching eyes always knew it,
before the dullness of the Great Domestication set in.
I do want more.
It's that simple.
You may think this cruel
if you have already fallen in love with habit.

"Even your house of love
will be shattered and swept away
by the tide of Love itself – and without apology –
to become an anthropologist's artifact,
an interesting study of how an earlier love
was constructed.
Do you see now?
I want to transcend myself
in you.

"Befriend fear,
that unsolicited angel
appearing at the tent
of your life,
come to announce
that the Wild One
is breaking camp and moving on.
Time to pull up stakes.
Again.
Nobody (not the Nazarene for sure)
said it would be easy.
Here's my one concession
to your fear:
Lean back.
I will carry you for a time
in the momentum of my yearning.
The Future asks – only – for your trust."

In John's gospel, Jesus' encounter with Nicodemus is the clearest illustration that Jesus prized the capacity to move and be moved by the Spirit as the surest sign of being "born from above": "The wind blows where it chooses, and you hear the sound of it, but you do not know where it comes from or where it goes. So it is with everyone who is born of the Spirit" (John 3:8).

My reading of the New Testament tells me that the nomadic Jesus was anti-temple, anti-sacrificial, anti-empire, and anti-religion-as-obedience to external law. His overthrowing of the merchant tables in the temple was a symbolic overthrowing of the temple itself, and of the commercialization of the sacrificial practices of the temple, which preyed on the poor.

Whereas his own religion had confused morality and obedience with the spiritual impulse to evolve, and while the Roman Empire tried to build a mono-lithic culture of "little Romes" when they conquered a new city, Jesus seemed to channel a creative power that was wild, unpredictable, and iconoclastic.

His life more closely reflected the prophecy of Jeremiah, who envisioned the day when the Law would be written upon the hearts of the people (Jeremiah 33:31–33). The old covenant is distinguished from Jeremiah's new covenant as a shift from a hand-holding immaturity to a G_d-knowing maturity: "It will not be like the covenant that I made with their ancestors when I took them by the hand to bring them out of the land of Egypt" (31:32).

In the old days, G_d took "the ancestors" *by the hand* to lead them into a kind of freedom – a political form of freedom. Freedom "from" the Egyptians. But the inner spiritual freedom was still coming, waiting to be realized. This is a freedom that includes the "from" dimension, but it is also "for" something – the something that was imagined in the freeing from. My best guess is that it's a comprehensive freedom, which includes the political, social, and economic, but which flows from an interior condition wherein one is liberated, moment by moment, to respond intuitively to the promptings of Spirit. Those who follow a nomadic G_d must be themselves nomadic, spontaneous, and liberated from consensus reality.

You can see the evolution of freedom in this covenant. It is born of knowing G_d directly and immediately, a mystic knowing. There will be no hand-holding. We can think of hand-holding as strict obedience to a set of external or internal laws for fear of punishment. This is an immature form of obedience, absolutely necessary at a particular stage of spiritual development. Children who haven't internalized the laws, morals, and rules of how to behave in public absolutely need hand-holding. They need to be taught what is right and wrong, and to be praised and rewarded for doing what is right.

This is, of course, what Paul experienced in his shift from the hand-holding covenant of the Law to the "new" covenant of being "in Christ." The "hand-holding" covenant can be experienced within any religion, including Christianity. When members of a congregation look exclusively to the wisdom of "the minister," and when a belief system is absolutized, the religion that forms around it consists in "hearing *about*" G_d from some other authority. At that point, the hand-holding old covenant is operating – versus the active cultivation of the individual and community's capacity to know G_d directly.

When the outer law becomes the inner, spiritual law (that is, when we know it to be "written on our hearts"), the new covenant is enacted. This involves learning to trust and validate one's own experience and to interpret one's own experience.

The Jesuit spiritual teacher Jean-Pierre de Caussade (1675–1751) wrote about "the sacrament of the present moment," when every moment and every event, no matter how mundane, is potentially an opening to G_d. He teaches that we must be ready, willing, and able to respond to the promptings of Spirit. This practice assumes that the divine covenant is not only written upon *our* hearts, but penetrates and permeates the whole universe, Earth, and nature with wisdom. It is written into the movement of the stars, the cycles of the moon, and the seasons of the year. It is written upon the hearts of our kin creatures. And when we evolve into the heart covenant, we participate in the heart covenant of the entire universe. This is the universal wisdom (Sophia) that Proverbs, Sirach, Baruch, and Job witness to. Sophia herself is said to be "more mobile than motion" (Wisdom 7:24). And this is the Wisdom, according to the Christian lineage, that took form in Jesus of Nazareth, nomad of the new covenant.

The new covenant, as it is expressed in evolutionary spirituality, states that what was written about and believed about Jesus for the past 2,000 years, was a necessary projection onto him of our own human potential. We needed a Jesus of Nazareth in order to see all this potential externalized. We needed first to be able to see all this potential *outside* of ourselves. Jesus became a living icon, and through contemplation, we become that which we contemplate. If we were to leave this projection in place, and claim that only in Jesus can these potentials be realized, we would be living out of the old, hand-holding covenant.

But it is well past time that we withdrew the projection so that our *own* hearts might be animated by the living wisdom that lit up his precious soul. No teachers will be needed, because people will have direct access to a heart-wisdom. No rulebooks will be required; no, "we've always done it this way" kind of thinking. I'm pretty sure that if Jesus were alive today he would look upon the fundamentalist reduction of Christianity to shallow moralism and shake his head. He would be baffled that given his own anti-sacrificial stance, he himself was understood to be G_d's human sacrifice! He would be dismayed by a church that excludes gays, lesbians, and transsexuals simply on the basis of sexual orientation. The "law" that is written upon our hearts is not a law carved on tablets of stone. It is, I suggest, more like the law of evolution, which is a continual process of self-transcendence.

Jesus embodied the new covenant. This is what caused the writer of Mark's gospel to say of the authorities of Jesus' day, "The people were amazed at his teaching, because he taught them as one who had authority, not as the teachers of the law" (Mark 1:22, NIV). Not, that is, as one who was simply passing on what he had heard from others. This is what made Jesus so compelling, so threatening, and so hard to pin down. And this is the goal for all who follow in the lineage of Jesus – to become self-authorizing individuals and self-authorizing communities.

The "call" stories in the New Testament are dramatic. They depict Jesus calling one disciple after another, each of whom drops his life and follows Jesus. I once thought these stories must be hyperbole. Today, I'm not so sure. Your soul, and mine, lives to be awakened by reality, by a love that we each came to collect on. In fact, most of us grow into adulthood deeply disappointed by life. What disappoints us most, I believe, is ourselves. Love comes like a Nazarene peasant to us all at some point, and invites us to follow. If, because of fear, we turn down that invitation and follow the voice of conventional culture, which is organized around other values, our souls fall into slumber. Or they go missing in action. To be lit up by the call of a nomad is to be willing to drop everything that impedes our moving with him, and moving within a universe that is itself on the move.

Jesus as shaman and mystic

Mircea Eliade writes, "no religion is completely 'new', no religious message completely abolishes the past. Rather, there is a recasting, a renewal, a revalorization, an integration of the elements – the most essential elements! – of an immemorial religious tradition."[6]

Ideally, the most essential and true elements of an "immemorial religious tradition" are carried forward and integrated into any new religion. From my reading of the New Testament, somehow Jesus carried forward the essential elements of shamanism. Unfortunately, Christianity in general has historically regarded the work of shamans as "witchcraft." The presence of shamanic priests no doubt threatened the priestly hierarchy of the church. The modernist worldview and bias, with its excessive rationalism and preference for empirically-based truth, has prevented us from incorporating the wisdom of shamanism – and therefore the wisdom of Jesus himself. We are mostly embarrassed by the witness of the New Testament and go to great rational lengths to explain miracles, exorcisms, apocalyptic utterances, and healing.

Progressive Christianity itself has become excessively rational and without access to the transrational our spirituality has become arid. We have lost our feel for the unseen realms, and therefore focus exclusively on the externals. Unless, for example, our commitment to social justice arises from knowledge of the realms that were available to Jesus, we become more of a social service agency.

The upshot is that the preponderance of stories in the New Testament that involve "miracles," exorcisms, telepathy, healing at a distance, and even soul retrieval are simply dismissed as the superstitious beliefs of a culture that did not have the benefit of a scientific worldview. After a lifetime of making these assumptions myself, I have now realized how reductionistic they are. They speak to the fact that our society has narrowed its vision down to the very small realm of the material. Progressive Christianity might allow for G_d, but other spiritual beings are mostly regarded as superstition.

Shamanism likely originated in the regions known today as Russia and Mongolia and is characterized by a direct awareness of spirit beings that are invisible to a conventional consciousness. Through trance and ritual, a shaman's consciousness opens up to these invisible realms. Shamans are set aside by a tribe to commune with these beings, along with the spirits of the dead

---

6   Mircea Eliade, *Shamanism: Archaic Techniques of Ecstasy*, (Princeton: Princeton University Press, 1964), 12.

(the ancestors), and to provide healing for the community as a whole, and for individuals. They are able to travel to the lower, middle, and upper realms in order to retrieve lost souls.

Jesus is portrayed as an exorcist, but we should get images from *The Exorcist* off our minds. It's not about spinning heads. Exorcists cast out entities that have taken up residence where they do not belong. The story of the Gerasene demoniac is an example of Jesus as shaman, exorcising on both an individual and social level (Mark 5:1–17). The man is screaming and running naked throughout the countryside. The demons offer their name as Legion. The name is no accident. A legion of the Roman Empire could have as many as 6,000 fighting men. Legion is the violent, occupying spirit of the Roman Empire, "possessing" the nation of Israel. It needed to be cast out in order for Israel (along with the man) to be restored to health. Jesus sends the demons into pigs (an unclean animal), which run headlong over a cliff into the sea.

Shamans also perform soul-retrievals. When a person is traumatized, part of the soul may split off and move into a different realm. If it is not reunited, then sickness can result. Shamans are able to travel to the lower realms to retrieval these alienated aspects of soul. One thinks here of the parables of the lost sheep and the lost coin, and the ultimate importance of retrieving the lost one. It's not only the marginalized of society that Jesus came to bring back into the fold, which is the assumption that drives much of the work around social justice. That work is important. But equally important is the interior work of retrieving the part of the soul lost through trauma. As shaman, Jesus knew how to do this.

One thinks, as well, of the story of Jesus healing the young girl who was said to be already dead. Jesus asks people to wait outside. (Most shamans work alone with the patient.) He tells them that she is not dead, but sleeping. He goes in, takes her hand, and says, "Little girl, get up!" (Mark 5:41). From a shamanic perspective, he connected with the little girl's soul and brought her back from the dead.

The tradition has it that, after his death, Jesus visited the imprisoned: "He was put to death in the flesh, but made alive in the spirit, in which also he went and made a proclamation to the spirits in prison…" (1 Peter 3:19). The context makes it clear that this visit wasn't to a literal prison, but to those souls who were cut off from G_d after they died. As well, in the Apostles Creed, the tradition is that on Holy Saturday, after the crucifixion, Jesus visited hell to redeem souls, or to "loose their souls" so that they could return to the Father: "Jesus was crucified under Pontius Pilate, died, and was buried. He descended into the dead." I am convinced that these traditions are grounded in the memory of an earlier spiritual lineage of shamanism.

Personal friend, contemporary shaman, and Anglican priest Chris Dierkes describes what's going on in these passages as "psychopomp":

> Psychopomps are journeys where a shaman meets a soul in a postmortem state who is unable to cross over into the other world. This soul is stuck in between the worlds, often confused, in pain, and alone. The shaman, acting as psychopomp, helps the soul: a) realize it is in fact dead b) clear any remaining ties that bind the soul to this world c) encourage the soul to make the journey across the dividing line between this world and the hereafter.[7]

A truly progressive religion of the 21st century will endeavour to include the deep intelligence and wisdom of the shamanic and mystic lineage, which undoubtedly informed Jesus' own orientation. We must become transrational in our approach and in what we teach our adherents if we are to be anything other than a social service agency.

---

7 http://beamsandstruts.com/articles/item/1014-jesus-the-shaman

―――― SIX ――――

Jesus as the Son of Man

Human beings are made not born.
— Stephen Jenkinson, founder of Orphan Wisdom

I have separated out a particular image of Jesus from the images in the previous chapter for emphasis. In part, I do this because it is a biblical image that has been virtually ignored by scholarship. And I do it as well because, as we'll see, it is the one title that Jesus identified with himself.

It is curious that scholarship, with a few notable exceptions, has virtually ignored the one title that Jesus himself may have identified with – the "son of man." In the Greek, the article is included making the literal translation "the son of *the* man." I will use the translation "the son of the Human One," "Human One," or "True Human."

The phrase is used in the Hebrew scriptures 108 times, 93 of them in Ezekiel. It is used in the New Testament 87 times. There are a total of 53 different sayings in which it is used. I am indebted, here, to the wonderful work of New Testament scholar Walter Wink, and his book *The Human Being: Jesus and the Enigma of the Son of Man*.

As Wink points out, Jesus rejected the titles "Messiah," son of God, or God at various times. (This, of course, didn't stop the church from giving him these titles after his death.) But the one title Jesus *did* apply to himself was "son of the Human One." Most scholars conclude that this was simply his way of referring to himself in the third person, but they never explained why he would do this, and it wasn't common in the Aramaic language to do so. In fact, Jesus frequently uses "I" when referring to himself. It seems clear that Jesus had something else in mind when he used this title to refer to himself.

The Human One connotes a transcendent dimension of what it means to be human – transcendent and yet within our G_d-given capacity to realize: human, but not by virtue of mere biological birth. The True Human results from a transformation. This is consistent with Jesus saying in the gospel of John that we must be born of water *and* Spirit. In indigenous cultures, we will see that this transcendent dimension was brought about through initiation rituals.

The transcendent human of Ezekiel's vision

But the place to begin unravelling the meaning of the Human Being is Ezekiel's vision of the divine throne chariot (Ezekiel 1:26–28, English Standard Version).

> And above the expanse over their heads there was the likeness of a throne, in appearance like sapphire; and seated above the likeness of a throne was a likeness with a human appearance. And upward from what had the appearance of his waist I saw as it were gleaming metal, like the appearance of fire enclosed all around. And downward from what had the appearance of his waist I saw as it were the appearance of fire, and there was brightness around him. Like the appearance of the bow that is in the cloud on the day of rain, so was the appearance of the brightness all around. Such was the appearance of the likeness of the glory of the Lord.

The remarkable revelation of this vision is that God appears to Ezekiel *as* human. I take this to mean that God is showing Ezekiel that realizing the divine image within means becoming human, and becoming human is the realization of the divinity for those of us born as human beings.

It is important to recognize that in Ezekiel's vision God is not *only* human. God appears in this vision in the form of other animals as well. It makes sense that in being a giraffe, the giraffe has fulfilled its purpose, that is, it has realized the divine image for its species. The difference between a human and a giraffe is that once a giraffe reaches adulthood its evolution stops. Humans are the species who never stop becoming, or at least who have the potential to perpetually expand their consciousness and participate in the emergence of new cultures. This is our glory, our privilege, and our responsibility.

Humans as the missing link to the Human

To become fully human is to realize the divine image within us – the divine appearing in human form. There is much talk in some religious lineages and in New Age spirituality about our goal being to transcend humanity and become divine. Third-century theologian and bishop Athanasius is often interpreted as having written, "G_d became human so that humans could become divine." But I agree with Wink that the sacred vocation of humans is to realize our humanity. We realize our humanity by transcending our humanity – in the process of *becoming* Human – and this happens multiple times in the course of a well-lived life, a life that is open to becoming.

This transcendence involves not merely a restoration back to some presumed original essence and goodness, but actually a pressing forward, to use Paul's phrase, to realize undiscovered potentials. Repentance, in this model, is not for the purpose of recovering from Original Sin, but rather it is turning away from all the cultural norms, all the personal and historical trauma, and all limiting belief systems that hypnotize us and that keep us from realizing our humanity, which is, as we've also seen, our divinity, our sacred vocation.

I am reminded here of the original meaning of the Greek word *metanoia*. Most often it is translated as "conversion" or "repentance." But the deeper meaning goes beyond repentance. As noted earlier, the literal meaning is "higher mind." The goal is not merely to repent of sin. Mere repentance, without adopting a higher mind – higher than the one that was the source of our original mistake – leads to a lifetime of repetition. Einstein said that you can't get out of a problem with the same mind that got you into it. The evolutionary task of the True Human is to live from a higher mind and a more open heart than the one we now have.

New Testament scholar Gerd Theissen points out that paleoanthropologists have been looking for the missing evolutionary link between primates and humans. Only now are we realizing that *we* could be that missing link! "But human beings are an eschatological reality, the future, emergent work in progress, still well behind our realization."[1]

The ordeal of becoming human

We are steeped in the belief that by virtue of our birth we are human. But Stephen Jenkinson is right when he says that humans are made, not born. All indigenous cultures knew this. They knew that children, for example, needed to be initiated into adulthood. This involved a killing off of the child self, at the appropriate time, in a rigorous initiation ritual designed to help the child become the next iteration of the human being s/he was meant to be. Jenkinson is convincing in his assessment that North American contemporary culture is so narcissistic because we have no initiation ceremonies by which we kill off the child in order to grow the adult. Our collective narcissism shows up as either very low self-esteem (carrying on as though our presence on Earth doesn't matter) or grandiosity (carrying on as though the universe revolves around us).[2]

It is also true that *adults* need to undergo a death. This is a core message of Jesus and of Paul. We come into adulthood having formed our personalities as compensation patterns, as an unconscious and deeply necessary reaction to various traumas (both personal and cultural), failures of love, unconscious agreements, and all manner of unresolved issues in our family of origin. This personality or persona is the shell we present to the world. But over time, the shell of our personality actually prevents the kernel of life within (call it the soul) from connecting to the evolutionary life process, or the Source of All.

The shell of our personality is put in place to keep the shadow from overwhelming us. The shadow is all the buried truth, unconscious beliefs, motivations, and grief we carry in our unconscious. This all needs to crack open, whether through therapy, vision quests, plant medicine, or other modalities.

---

1 Gerd Theissen, *Biblical Faith: An Evolutionary Approach*, trans. J. Bowden (Philadelphia: Fortress Press, 1985), 122.

2 These ideas were shared during the course of a presentation given by Stephen.

Until we make a conscious decision to allow this to happen and avail ourselves of the opportunity we will not realize our humanity.

One thinks of the anemic confirmation rituals in most churches, which involve almost no ordeal (other than asking the adolescent confirmands to endure the boredom of the classes). This process seems to have as its goal initiating the child into the church culture and denomination, in the hope that this will get him or her to stick around. But our young people aren't sticking around and there is good reason. They want to be challenged. They want to be initiated into the cosmos, into the evolutionary adventure of the world, not into the church. They want to find and live from their soul. These kids want to know that the church is up to something. They are looking for mentorship, someone who will teach them what it means to be Human, and how to proceed in life as if they matter. Mentorship should not be confused with asking senior citizens to team up with a young person. Senior citizens who have not been initiated into the True Human can't be expected to mentor others just because they are older.

This aligns with the insight of the author of 1 John, when he wrote, "Beloved, we are God's children now; what we will be has not yet been revealed. What we do know is that when the Human One (he or it) is revealed, we will be like it, for we will see it as it is" (1 John 3:2, paraphrase). The promise here is that the sacred evolutionary trajectory – for those willing to die to their personas (again and again) – will transform us so completely that we will end up like the archetypal Human One. We will recognize that because we have become it!

The Human Being sitting on the throne, Ezekiel claims, is the appearance of the likeness of the glory of the Lord" (1:26). As we are in the process of becoming ourselves Human, G_d is being realized through us. As I've said, this doesn't mean that our goal is to transcend our humanness in order to become divine. Quite the contrary, our vocation is to inhabit our humanity more deeply and to catalyze the evolutionary creativity that is living us. In so doing, we reveal the glory of G_d.

Wink posits that around the time of Jesus, the Human Being of Ezekiel's vision was exerting an archetypal pressure on the consciousness of humanity in general, and in particular on Jesus. This archetype was awakened in Jesus to such an extent that he identified with it. His life was animated by the power of the archetype of the True Human. As the representative of the Human Being (son of the Human One), Jesus was activated to break open his own religious lineage to the evolutionary power that this archetype exerted. His life became about initiating others into their deep humanity. This would involve awakening others to their vocation of realizing their divine nature *as* Humans. Jesus was about "humanizing humanity."[3]

When I speak of archetypes or ideal forms, I do not mean to imply that there is only one form of the True Human that we are in the process of becoming. Humans, as a species, are precisely *not* determined, as is true for the inorganic and organic realms. We are the *determiners*, and it's important to say that we are *not* being determined by an archetype of the Human One. Rather, the archetype *itself* implies an evolution of our capacity for freedom to realize our uniqueness and individuality, in the context of interrelatedness.

It is typical in our culture, when referring to humanity, to reduce our species down to its most vulnerable, fragile, and failure-prone manifestation, captured in the phrase, "he's *only* human." When Jesus' human nature is referred to, it is always distinguished from his divine nature, or higher nature. "He was human, just like us," is a privileged mantra of liberal Christianity. He had doubts. He made mistakes. He made errors in judgment sometimes. This tendency is an understandable reaction to theologies that make Jesus out to be invulnerable, all-knowing, and perfect. It's hard to relate to perfection. But I believe that it's time to elevate Jesus' humanity, as Human One, as one who is animated by the full potential of the Human. This means a human being who is absolutely committed to exercising freedom to participate in the evolutionary process of becoming ever more human.

It was perhaps inevitable that when philosophers, theologians, and scientists began to integrate Darwin's evidence for evolution, it would be applied to

---

3   Walter Wink, *The Human Being: Jesus and the Enigma of the Son of Man* (St. Paul, Minnesota: Paragon House, 2007), 32.

anthropology, the study of what it means to human. This led to two broad and divergent streams of thought about the nature of humanity. Some found his theory that we are descendants of apes to be a shameful reduction of humanity, essentially reducing us to animals with bigger brains. If we are no more than thinking apes, why trust the thoughts of such a creature, and if nature usurps the traditional role of G_d, where does that leave faith? Some Christians, then and now, react strongly to this and reject the theory altogether. In contemporary culture, this takes the form of creationism (intelligent design).

For the other stream, Darwin's theory was cause for celebration and an almost giddy optimism about the future. If humans took this kind of exponential leap from apes, then surely the future human would far surpass the current form of human.

Nietzsche's "Superman" and Aurobindo's corrective

This led the German philosopher Friedrich Nietzsche to develop the metaphor of the übermensch, or "superman," as the future man. But for Nietzsche the superman undermined what he considered to be the weak ideals of the Christian religion. Here is a sampling of Nietzschean quotes about the superman:

> I teach you superman. Man is something that shall be surpassed. What
> have you done to surpass him…The superman is the meaning of Earth.
> Let your will say, the superman shall be the meaning of earth…Let the
> radiance of a star shine through your love! Let your hope be: May I give
> birth to the superman! O my brothers, what I can love in man is that he
> is a transition and a destruction. And in you too there is much that lets
> me love and hope.[4]

Nietzsche's superman, however, was the Titan, the strongman, the conquering man who triumphed over nature. Napoleon was his favourite model of the superman. The weakest would be weeded out as the superman emerged to rule

---

4 Friedrich Nietzsche, Introduction to *On Zarathustra*, vol. 75, p. 8, par. 3, as quoted in Ernest
   Benz, *Evolution and Christian Hope: Man's Concept of the Future* (London: Victor Gollancz
   Ltd., 1967), 109. Friedrich Nietzsche, Introduction to *On Zarathustra*, vol.75, p.8, par.3

the earth. This kind of thinking eventuated in eugenics, by which the weak would be systematically eliminated. Hitler, for example, saw the Jews as a race of people who were holding back the evolution of the human species.

This kind of thinking led to a generalized and understandable postmodernist backlash against any conversation about the progress of the human species. A young intern of biologist David Sloane Wilson tried to apply the insights of evolutionary theory to other fields. Wilson writes,

> He quickly learned that when he spoke of human behavior, psychology and culture in evolutionary terms, their minds churned through an instant and unconscious process of translation, and they heard "Hitler", "Galton", "Spencer", "IQ differences", "holocaust", "racial phrenology", "forced sterilization", "genetic determinism", "Darwinian fundamentalism", and "disciplinary imperialism."[5]

Sri Aurobindo also imagined that evolution was producing the superman, but his vision more closely reflected the Christian imagination for the Human One. He takes issue with Nietzsche precisely on this issue. Who is the superman for Aurobindo?

> The one who can rise above this matter-regarding, broken, mentally human unity, and present himself universalized and deified in a divine force, a divine love, and a divine knowledge. If thou keenest this limited human ego and thinkest thyself the superman, thou art but the fool of thy own pride, the plaything of thy own forces and the instrument of thy own illusions. Nietzsche was the superman as the lion soul passing out of camelhood, but the true heraldic divine and token of the superman is the lion seated upon the camel which stands on the cow of plenty. If thou canst not be the slave of all mankind thou art not fit to be his master, and if thou canst not make thy nature as Vasistha's cow of plenty, with all mankind to draw its wish from her udders, what avails

---

5 David Sloan Wilson, *The Literary Animal: Evolution and the Nature of Nature* (Evanston, IL: NorthWestern University Press, 2005), 20.

thy lionized supermanhood?[6]

Sri Aurobindo knew that the ego must be crucified, that the Titan within must rise up, yes, but then die to its own power and be the servant of all, in order to ascend to the status of the True Human.

There is much in evolutionary spirituality that tends towards the Nietzschean image of the superman. It is all too easy to get swept away by a vision of the transcendent human being, rising above all suffering and vulnerability, and unilaterally building the New Jerusalem. These utopian visions reflect what I call a theology of glory, which does not include the cross.

A comprehensive evolutionary spirituality, however, must incorporate the story of Jesus, which elicits a theology of fragility. This concept is best captured by an interview I heard between radio host Kristen Tippet and French geophysicist Xavier le Pichon.

Le Pichon was the first to get in a submersible and go down a couple of miles to the bottom of the sea. He saw these fault lines; they were the shifting tectonic plates. It's the first time humans realized that Earth's crust was in motion. He got so immersed in his science, that one day he realized that he was completely ignoring the suffering of the world. He walked away from science and went to work with Sr. Teresa in Calcutta. He held dying babies in his arms and promised that he would never abandon them. Then we went to live in a L'Arche community and met Jean Vanier. Jean Vanier told him absolutely live in community with them, but carry on with his science. It was too important to ignore.

Based on his work with tectonic plates, dying babies, and his opening to suffering, le Pichon developed a theology of fragility. The fault lines he discovered are the cause of tsunamis and earthquakes, as we know all too well, but they are also how Earth renews itself, with a fresh influx of minerals and chemicals from Earth's core. Earth's fragility and the fragility of the human condition, highlighted in his care for abandoned infants, made him realize that suffering had a purpose, which was the evocation of empathy. It's how the

6 Sri Aurobindo, *Thoughts and Aphorisms* (Sri Aurobindo Ashram, 1958), 22.

universe grows a heart. The broken heart is the fault line that evokes empathy.

As a Christian, le Pichon looked at the cross and saw it as a kind of fault line, a tectonic shift in the history of humanity that revealed the violence in the heart of humanity. But when we are willing to contemplate the cross deeply, it has the power to evoke empathy. In this broken body, the fragile places of the whole evolving story, from the death of stars to the suffering of species, to our own suffering, is gathered up as a divine empathic response to the suffering of creation. There is a revitalization that emerges from this cataclysmic event – an evolution of empathy. So the evolutionary purpose of suffering is the evocation and deepening of empathy.

Evolution proceeds – cosmologically, biologically, psychologically, culturally, and spiritually – in and through vulnerability and death, whether we're talking about a supernova, an extinction of massive proportions, or, in humans, a conscious purging of all that is not love, a dying to ego-driven motivations.

"But if we have died with Christ, we believe that we will also live with him" (Romans 6:8). Our vocation is to learn the delicate art of dying, over and over again – what Jesus referred to as "taking up the cross" and "dying in order to live." Emergence is staggeringly complex, and the most central practice is to remove roadblocks from the procession of grace, flowing from the heart of Creator.

Once we take seriously a theology of fragility as necessary to evolve our species along the empathic line of intelligence, there is room as well to integrate an aspirational ideal – we are truly wired for self-transcendence as a species. The church itself throughout history has produced leaders whose primary focus has been on the work of the Holy Spirit as elucidated in John's gospel: "Very truly, I tell you, the one who believes in me will also do the works that I do and, in fact, will do greater works than these, because I am going to the Father" (John 14:12).

This led a second-century, charismatic leader named Montanus to be the first to develop the idea of the human as superman.[7] By virtue of the Holy Spirit, what Aurobindo might call the descent of the "supermind," certain hu-

---

7 Benz, Evolution, 17–19.

mans were raised to a higher consciousness, a higher ethical responsibility, and higher competencies. Montanus does not even regard himself as one who has been saved in the traditional sense. By the Spirit he had been raised to the highest level of Human, transcending the need for salvation. He actually rejected salvation as being purely restorative – that is back to an original image of G_d within. It was his experience that salvation history was actually the story of humans transcending all former images. Salvation was an ongoing process for him, what today we might call conscious evolution, or in the passive voice, *being evolved* by Spirit.

In his book *Evolution and Christian Hope*, Ernest Benz points out that this kind of movement was actually quite common in the first two centuries of the church, but was elbowed out (sometimes more violently) by a theology (notably Augustine's) focused less on the extraordinary capacities of the person animated by the Holy Spirit, and more on the generalized grace and salvation available to the "common" or "average" human, through the mediation of the church and her priests.

After Darwin published *The Origin of Species*, a number of continental theologians were inspired by the vision of the superman. You can catch the anthropological Christology in the following words of Edgar Dacqué, who was a Protestant Christian and director of the Munich museum of paleontology.

> Thus the earthly man, sublime as his natural form may be, joins the
> rest of nature in expectation of perfect man who, in a new way, shall be
> the true image and facsimile of God. Present earthly man will become
> extinct and will be replaced by a new, more perfect man. In his inner-
> most being, he really 'aims' toward this new form of man, he carries it
> within himself, he wants to give expression to it, as subhuman nature
> once aimed for and was pregnant with him.[8]

Dacqué was convinced that something like the archetypal image of the Son of Man in Ezekiel's vision was embedded in all creation, from the Big Bang for-

8 Edgar Dacqué, *Urwelt, Sage, Menschheit*, 6th ed., 1931, as quoted in Benz, *Evolution*, 178.

ward. "Man's (sic) original form was therefore already metaphysically present in the organic kingdom…Although, chronologically speaking, as fully developed man, appeared only in the last period of the earth, he was already present in all living creatures, uncounted millions of years ago…"[9]

"Man," for Dacqué, was the original form out of which the rest of creation evolved and continues to evolve. The current form of humans is also temporary, containing within it the "Eternal Man." In time, this iteration of humanity will be transcended. What happened in Jesus will continue to happen through us until Eternal Man is born, which will be the culmination of history. Jesus of Nazareth was the foretaste of this end. Therefore humans are not the tip of tree of life emerging out of lower forms. Rather, the Human One is the original form that is shaping the tree of life itself.

Another German theologian, Leopold Ziegler, developed this understanding of the "Universal Man," which effects an evolutionary jump from current "man" to the superman. Noting that the "last, just-noticeable tendency of life is the mystical urge to transcend reality in its present form again and again," the superman appeared to him as an inevitable development. Furthermore, this future was already embedded in the current human being, and was waiting for realization. For Ziegler, this was the scriptural theology of promise and fulfillment.[10]

> Thus we saw Universal Man ascend from Universal Animal, or more
> precisely, *within* Universal Animal, of which, in a deeper sense, he was
> and is an "earlier stage". Universal Man is working irresistibly, all the
> time, as the cycles of theogony, cosmogony, and anthropology and there-
> fore as one single, continuous, forward, and backward manifestation of
> God, the universe, and man. By whatever name we call him, that carrier
> and mediator with the never-failing memory, whether we call him the
> restorer or the one who will arrive, standing up and floating in the air,

---

9 Ibid.

10 Leopold Ziegler, *Lehrgespräch vom Allgemeinen Menschen* (Hamburg, 1956), as quoted in Benz, *Evolution*, 188–189.

he will always merge into the image of the son of Man of revelation…I am the first and the last. I am the immemorial, the uninjured, and the injured. My body is in all that is corporeal; I am nailed on the cross with all flesh; my body is devoid of all corporeality. I am death and resurrection; I am transformation and life. I am the reversion, the return, and the homecoming. I am the reappearance and the restoration.[11]

A nuanced approach to the idea of the superman (and progress in general) requires that we balance a theology of glory and the more extraordinary capacities available to humans with a theology of fragility and vulnerability. We also need to recognize that it is not inevitable that the future will be more glorious. The evolutionary thrust of the universe towards an increase in complexity, consciousness, and compassion, can be cooperated with, or it can be thwarted. There is no grand design. The future truly is open and requires us, as the presence of the evolution that has become conscious of itself, to make courageous choices about the future.

Philippians 2:6–7 contains the earliest Christian hymn portrayal of Jesus as one who was in the form of G_d, but who did not cling to that status. Rather, Jesus emptied himself, "taking the form of a servant." *Kenosis* is the Greek word that is translated as "emptied." The Human of the future will be realized through a process of self-emptying, non-grasping, and deep trust that the Wholeness that is living us is best served by removing all obstacles, the biggest one of which is, more often than not, our own self.

The Christology of humanity
Lo, I tell you a mystery:
God is Human, and we are to become like God.
– Walter Wink

What Nietzsche reacted so strongly against was a pervasive passivity that he saw in the Christian religion. When blind obedience to the will of G_d, along with the understanding of faith as believing the right things, is overempha-

---

11 Ibid., 253.

sized, human potential is diminished. When passive carrying out of the orders of a transcendent G_d eliminates the active, creative agency of the human being as a co-creator, it can result, for example, in acquiescence to the religious and political status quo.

Russian theologian and philosopher Nikolai Berdyaev (1874–1948)[12] articulates a view of the human being that balances the passive and active dimensions of the life journey. We do need to feel, on the one hand, that we are being lived by a Wholeness that transcends our individual ego and be willing to radically entrust our lives to this power. This is the passive end of the continuum. On the other hand, we are creatures who have been given the gift of creativity. This means that the Logos, Word, or Creative Principle that is incarnating a world, us included, is now creating in, through, and as the human being.

To use an analogy from the parable of the sower, the human being is the sower, the seed, and the soil – all three. As the sower, we scatter our seed (creativity). As the seed, we need to be willing to allow the husk of the seed (our personality) to be cracked open. We need to be willing to die to all that is keeping us from life in every moment. As the soil, we need to be actively cultivating our inner life so that we can be fertile ground for the evolutionary process to continue through us.

To deny our own creativity is to become ourselves an obstacle to the Spirit-animated evolutionary process. G_d is now creating *in, through,* and *as* us! We are, effectively, the Word (seed) made flesh. The early church recognized this in Jesus, and it is true of us as well.

Berdyaev came up with the metaphor of the "anthropological revelation," which is essentially the revealing of the True Human. The future coming of the Human One "with great power and glory" (Mark 13:26) wasn't about Jesus' long awaited return. Rather, it was about the activation on a general level (you and me) of the archetype of the Human One coming to reveal humanity's Christological nature. If this sounds radical, it is, in the way that it reverses conventional thinking about the Son of Man as Jesus, and the hope for his return

---

12 Wink, *The Human Being*, 47–48.

one day. Summarizing Berdyaev's theology, Wink writes, "The Coming Christ will come only to humanity which courageously accomplishes a Christological self-revelation, that is, reveals *in its own nature* divine power and glory."[13]

As far as Berdyaev was concerned, he saw a lot of false humility and self-righteous servility among Christians. But nowhere in the gospels is Jesus portrayed in this light. He was powerful. He was creative. He proclaimed bold things about the future. He lived on the edge. He risked his life for the new future that he proclaimed. He took on the powers and the principalities. He revealed the True Human, and his own humanity revealed his Christological nature, an essence that is not confined to him.

It's very important that we are able, at this point, to distinguish between Jesus, the man, and the Christ. The Christ is the creative principle, or the personalized presence of the principle of creative transformation, that is animating the whole universe and holding it all together. As we exercise our own creativity, love deeply, and live our lives fully moment to moment in freedom, we realize our own Christological nature *as human beings.* We, too, are that principle of creative transformation (the Word made flesh). We are the ones in whom the Human One or Future Human is exerting the tug of transcendence.

The author of John's gospel understood the implications of this deeply when he affirmed that Jesus' followers would do greater things than Jesus had done (John 14:12).

The writer of the gospel of Thomas also understood that it is not the calling of Christians to simply copy what Jesus did, or to believe that it is already accomplished. Rather, we are to be transformed to such a degree that we are animated by the same power that animated him: "When you make the two one, you will become Truly Human Beings ("sons of men"), and when you say, 'Mountain, move away,' it will move away" (Gospel of Thomas 106).

Making the "two one" can be understood as overcoming the illusion that there is me over here, and then there is the Word/Creative Principle out there somewhere, and that my vocation as a human being is to passively await the ac-

---

13 Ibid., 257.

tion of some external source of creativity. No. The Word has become flesh in me, in you, and in us together. The two are one. I am That. You are That. We are That.

> The Christological revelation, centered in Jesus, was that God desired to become incarnate in humanity. The anthropological revelation, not yet consummated, is that God has destined, or at least called us, to become human as *God* is human. We can redefine divinity, not as superhuman, post-human, or godlike, but more fully as what we already are: human beings.[14]

I would tweak Wink here just a bit by saying "what we already are" *potentially*: human beings. The fundamental role of church in the new age of Spirit must be to take seriously the task of initiation. The church (but not only the church) has been entrusted with the task of making of humans, or of "humanizing humanity." Or as Teilhard de Chardin put it, "christifying" humanity. In fulfilling this vocation, the church is called to go forward with the assumption that, as we do so, G_d is realizing G_dself in human form, and that our engagement with this fundamental vocation is prompted by G_d's own longing to be realized.

It is apparent by this point that the Human One, from my perspective, is the evolving Human. This is the human who has become aware *of* and consciously participates *in* an evolutionary impulse for transcendence – transcendence not *away* from the human condition, but to become ever more human.

The evolving human is the evolving mystic. Her reverence and respect for cosmos, Earth, biosystems, all species, and all previous human cultures arises naturally from the mystic awareness that these physical forms and cultural intelligences are very much alive and animating her in the present, and, through her, continue to shape the future.

The loss in modern culture of this intuitive awareness of radical interbeingness is the source of much modern illness and ecological disaster. When we participate as humans in the emergent future, with this mystic awareness

---

14 Ibid., 259.

and this deep reverence, we do so with greater wisdom. Without this awareness, respect, and reverence, we create the future as alienated supermen who will be incapable of producing anything but deeper alienation.

——— SEVEN ———

The Kin(g)dom of G_d

Spirituality is intimacy with a living universe.
— Duane Elgin

The central metaphor and the very heart of Jesus' teaching is the kin(g)dom of God. The term appears 162 times in the New Testament. Matthew uses the term kin(g)dom of Heaven, but it has the same meaning. There is no scholarly consensus about its meaning. Jesus never defined it, assuming that his hearers were familiar with it. The Aramaic word *malkuth*, which is translated as kingdom in the prayer of Jesus ("Your kingdom come"), refers not to any geographical location, but to the reign of God in history. It's what the world – its social, political, and economic systems – our communities, and our individual lives look like when love reigns. That is, when love, not the many forms of idolatry that humans offer their allegiance to, reigns.

Much has been written about how this may have been an intentionally subversive metaphor, contrasting the kin(g)dom of God with the Kingdom of Caesar. The latter was established through violence and privileged the powerful through the exercise of domination by force. The former is established through justice, non-violently privileging the marginalized through the exercise of vulnerable, self-giving love.

It may be that Jesus was declaring that *with* him, *in* him, and *through* him the kin(g)dom of God had arrived, and yet it awaited full realization in the future. In an evolutionary context, he embodied the Wholeness and the Health that is always, already present and waiting to be realized as future possibility for all humanity, and through humans, for the whole cosmos. He was the willing public exemplar for what the kin(g)dom of God looks like for humanity – which did not resemble what Caesar was doing nor what the prevailing religious authorities were doing. Jesus was critical of both, but particularly the latter. It is possible that he expected violence, corruption, and oppression of the poor from the worldly Caesar, but from his own lineage he expected much more and held the representatives to a different standard.

Idolatry and Owen Barfield

Owen Barfield (1898–1997) was a philosopher, poet, critic, and philologist. He had a deep intuition that the Christian tradition needed to come to terms with evolution as a driving force of the universe, but not neo-Darwinian evolution that reduces all of reality to matter. He was concerned particularly with the evolution of consciousness, and the way in which consciousness precedes, interacts, and indwells matter. Matter, in his philosophy and theology, is manifest spirit.

In the last chapter of his book *Saving Appearances: A Study in Idolatry,* he offers a particularly compelling take on the kin(g)dom of God, through the lens of idolatry. He points out that between Jesus' parable of the sower and his private interpretation of the parable for the disciples, the writer of Matthew's gospel inserts an important Old Testament allusion after the disciples ask him why he speaks in parables.

> You will indeed listen, but never understand, and you will indeed look, but never perceive. For this people's heart has grown dull, and their ears are hard of hearing, and they have shut their eyes; so that they might not look with their eyes and listen with their hearing, and understand with their heart and turn…" (Matthew 13:14–15).

This is almost a direct quote from Isaiah 6. But if we track this saying further, we discover that it takes us to Psalm 115:

> Their idols are silver and gold, the work of human hands. They have mouths, but do not speak; *eyes but do not see. They have ears, but do*

not hear... Those who make them are like them; so are all who trust in them" (vs. 4–8).

The parable is called by Jesus a "word of the kin(g)dom" in 13:24, and what prevents listeners from hearing and entering the kin(g)dom of God in a transformative way is idolatry. (Idolatry is what keeps the seed from falling into good soil and multiplying.) These images, claimed the prophets, were empty and lifeless – merely physical creations of humans, but treated like gods nevertheless. The prophets thereby emptied nature of the sovereign G_d, who was above all supposed nature gods, and wholly other than His creation. In this they anticipated the modernist project of scientific materialism, which again emptied matter of an interior, subjective dimension. Those who create idols, claims the psalmist, will become just like them – empty and lifeless. "Those who make them are like them; so are all who trust in them" (vs. 8).

But Jesus wasn't concerned with the kind of idolatry that the Old Testament prophets railed against, that is, the worship of graven images as numinous and holy. The new idolatry of the age and that Jesus challenged had been transferred from physical idols of a previous age to the human realm of slavish obedience to laws, holiness codes, dietary regulations, and other rituals that *replaced* rather than *reflected* the presence of Spirit. In other words, the new idolatry was a narrow moralism supported by a system of external laws for every aspect of life. The spiritual life as a radical trust in a living, nomadic G_d, present in every moment, was replaced by an idolatrous edifice.

Jesus criticized the religious authorities so severely because they were engaged in a new form of idolatry that he was exposing. The practice, the idolatry, was empty and meaningless on the one hand, but on the other these leaders laid an enormous and unnecessary burden upon the average person. To use Barfield's language, these external displays of piety did not participate *in*, nor were they participated *by*, Spirit.

It is interesting to note that almost all of Jesus' kin(g)dom teachings are followed by this injunction: "Those who have ears to hear (or eyes to see) let them hear (or see)." Jesus' kin(g)dom teachings were intended to take a person

- from emptiness to abundance
- from external displays of piety to inner and secret listening for Spirit
- from death to life
- from surface to a depth dimension
- from obedience to external authority to numinous and direct participation in Wisdom
- from anxious attachment to wealth to radical trust in Spirit
- from blindness to Spirit to seeing with luminous and sacramental awareness
- from fragmentation and alienation to wholeness and health.
- from ignorance and unconsciousness to alertness or conscious awareness.

You could say that to enter the kin(g)dom of God one was required to have some capacity for an interior life, for conscious self-awareness, and the ability to orient in life from self-authorization. One needed to be or to become a mystic. There is a shift from seeing through a lens of fragmentation and alienation to seeing the Wholeness that is animating and living all of life. Even in this midst of suffering, disease, and oppression, this Wholeness, for those with eyes to see, is waiting to be realized – symbolized in the gospels by the prevalence of healing stories.

Jesus saw the Wholeness (G_d) and enabled the sick, lame, blind, and diseased to participate in it. He called it "faith." "Your faith has made you well." But it wasn't faith *in* Jesus per se. It was the faith *of* Jesus. Faith as a way of seeing, of coming into coherence with, and manifesting the Wholeness. It was faith in whatever it was that Jesus was channelling. People saw Wholeness flowing through Jesus and in his presence they made Wholeness bigger than and more real than their illness. If we do not see it, we cannot participate in it, and thus we will be vulnerable to idolatry in its many forms.

But this requires a new way of seeing, as we've discovered. To enter the kin(g)dom of God we must be able to see and privilege Wholeness. Physicist Henri Bortoft talks about the part being the place for the presencing of the whole. What he means is that every individual, whether human or other than human, is the place that presences the Whole. Theologically speaking, we would say that the G_d is the Wholeness that is present in every aspect/part of the universe. When we are aligned with – that is, if we have "eyes to see" – this Wholeness, we do what the universe does naturally. We evolve.

When Jesus saw an ill person, he saw the Wholeness or the Health in the person. The symptoms he was confronted with were the way that the Wholeness was manifesting. They were the presenting clues as to where and how the Wholeness was being blocked or interfered with by incoherence or chaos. Disease, then, is not the absence of wholeness, but rather the way in which the Wholeness presents itself so that we have enough information to re-establish a natural coherence with it.

Idolatry prevents us from seeing and participating in the Wholeness because we grant absolute status to the part, rather than to the Wholeness itself. When we have symptoms of illness, for example, it is possible for the illness to take over our whole identity. Do *we* have cancer or does cancer have us? If the latter, then the part (cancer) is more than simply a symptom that shows us we are out of balance, along with our food, water, and farming systems. It has overtaken our identity. In Jesus' day, they called this "possession by demons." Foreign identities had usurped the sovereignty of the individual and needed to be cast out.

The allopathic medical system prevalent today is idolatrous in the way that it treats symptoms and not the whole person. This is to be expected since modern medicine is itself an expression of the idolatry of scientific materialism, which is fixated on treating the parts (physics, matter, chemistry) *as* the whole person. Modern medicine does so because of an assumption that the individual is nothing more than the sum of all the parts that comprise her body. You piece together all the aggregate parts and you get, not a whole, but a heap. This is totalism, not wholism.

In a *non*-materialistic paradigm, the body is merely the external aspect of a fathomless interiority. With wholism, the whole animates every part, and each part contains the whole. We are our emotions, values, beliefs, energy systems, soul, and ultimate we are a manifestation of the Whole which is Spirit. Scientific materialism and modern medicine, then, are living out of a "flat-land" view of the world that has no depth, no interiority.

If you look at the images that Jesus uses to describe the kin(g)dom of God, you will find that true life is discovered within a hidden depth dimension, which then manifests in the outer world. When the outer world of an individual, community, or society is animated by this depth dimension, it is living from Spirit. When it isn't, it is idolatrous. It is death parading as life, foolishness parading as wisdom, emptiness parading as abundance.

An obvious example is the seed, a favorite image of Jesus. If you confuse the outer shell with the whole seed, including the germ (the part for the Whole), you would be missing the mystery, or what Jesus called the mystery of the kin(g)dom. For the real potential lies in the kernel. To activate its potential, the shell must be buried deep in good enough soil, then under the right conditions, the hidden potential of the germ, found in the depths, sprouts to life.

For Jesus, the emphasis placed on dietary laws, purity codes, and Sabbath-keeping rules were very much like confusing the true life of Spirit (the kernel) with the shell of a seed. When people were forced to go through the religious motions, they were living like shells, never really opening up to the potential that lay deep within. The life they lived *looked good, it may even have sounded good,* but for those with ears to hear and eyes to see, it was idolatrous. These external actions were not a response to the life of the soul, which is connected to Spirit, but rather an impediment. This is why Jesus taught that the seed must die. The husk must be shed. The religious life as obedience to external laws must be shed, and the personality that adheres to this way of life must go to the cross with him, in order to rise with him a new creation.

The walking dead

As Isaiah's prophecy predicted, those who create and maintain the idols become themselves like the idols, empty and lifeless, parading around as representatives of a G_d they cannot feel within and do not know in their depths: "Woe to you, scribes and Pharisees, hypocrites! For you are like whitewashed tombs, which on the outside look beautiful , but inside they are full of the bones of the dead and of all kinds of filth" (Matthew 23:27).

This pithy, graphic image strikes at the heart of the matter. Death is death, no matter how you dress it up. Idolatry is living superficially and believing that this is all there is. It is hallowing the hollow. The schlock coming out of Hollywood, Disneyland, corporate media, the beauty and automobile industries, and consumerist culture in general is the contemporary equivalent of the whitewashed tombs to which Jesus referred. It all looks beautiful, sensational, and dramatic on the outside, but look inside and you'll find only the bones of the dead.

The rise of "zombie" iconography in popular culture reflects our whitewashed reality. Our artists are beginning to realize that we are zombies; living as superficially as we do, we have become the walking dead. We only *appear* to be human on the outside. Dissociated from what makes a human truly human – conscious alertness, soul, spirit, and heart – we merely zombies, grotesque caricatures of humans. The violence we are doing to our souls by focusing on externals, by seeing ourselves merely as consumers in an economic system that is deified, manifest in acts of outer violence perpetrated on Earth and her creatures, and upon ourselves. Zombies epitomize the end game of a consumer identity, that is, we consume each other.

Images of the Kin(g)dom: leaven and yeast

Jesus also uses the image of leaven (yeast) to describe the kin(g)dom of God. Leaven or yeast is a fungus that converts the sugars in the dough into carbon dioxide gas, which causes the bread to rise (and taste pretty darn good). In Jesus' day, yeast wasn't necessarily a good thing. At Passover, for example, the bread was to be unleavened, memorializing the escape from Egypt, when the Jews had no time for wait for the yeast to work.

Jesus warned his disciples against the "yeast" of the Pharisees and Sadducees (Matthew 16:6). Bad teachings just as much as good teachings act like yeast, activating and catalyzing the substance of the individual.

But on one occasion Jesus uses leaven in its positive meaning: "He told them another parable. 'The kingdom of heaven is like leaven that a woman took and hid in three measures of meal, till it was all leavened'" (Matthew 13:33, *New King James Version*).

Many translations of this one-line parable use the word "mixed" rather than "hid," but the latter gets at the mystical principle that there lives within us and within all of reality a hidden, "deep withinness" that is always active, but that is not visible and therefore not always recognized. One candidate for this principle that is hidden deep within and so close to us that we rarely notice it is the evolutionary current that compels us, and through us the cosmos, toward self-transcendence. It is, as we've seen, the potential for life hidden within matter; it is the potential for conscious self-awareness hidden with life; it is the spirit hidden within all.

Employing the image of yeast negatively, it becomes the idolatry that catalyzes unconscious commitment to the establishment, loyalty to the religious institution and its empty rituals and outward displays of piety. Idolatry causes us to offer our deepest allegiance to outer forms, to appearances, and to habitual re-enactments of history.

On the positive side, as a kin(g)dom image, the yeast that Jesus is talking about, this spirit-infused evolutionary current, gives rise to the spiritual freedom to create new futures, to participate in the "new way" that G_d is always creating for those with ears to ear and eyes to see. This new way, which is the future now, is the iconoclastic presence of Love fulfilling itself in and through our lives.

Teilhard de Chardin wrote frequently about a quality of life he called "zest." He was referring to the charge we can receive from the evolutionary current itself, which is driving toward self-transcendence. This, for Teilhard, is the Holy Spirit.

> The Holy Spirit is the power that makes evolution something more
> than a Darwinian play of necessity and accident. It is the force
> through which evolution becomes the awakening of spirit in matter…
> The Holy Spirit is active in the process of evolution from inorganic to

organic matter, and from mere organic matter to the life of ever higher life forms.[1]

We can see in his theological vision how the Holy Spirit could be understood as the yeast or leaven that activates the whole evolutionary process toward fulfillment. Above all, it was his contention that we needed to steward this zest, this catalyzing agent of the evolutionary impulse, in order to realize the kin(g)dom of God.

Jesus' image of yeast as a catalyzing agent describes this capacity that is built into the universe, and therefore into the human condition, to rise above current self-imposed limitations, perspectives, unconscious assumptions and beliefs, in order to leaven the ongoing development of the whole cosmos. Yeast is a compelling image for the science of cosmology, for we now know that the universe is indeed expanding in every direction from within – like a loaf of leavened bread!

The religious life of Jesus' own Jewish community, the life of the temple and of the priesthood, was overly focused on exteriors. The interior, subjective life of Spirit that animates all creation – let us call it the container of conscious awareness – was not informing or animating these rituals and laws. This is why Jesus challenged them with his teaching that the law (and the Sabbath) was made for humans, and not the reverse. Humans were not made to serve these inanimate structures and norms (Mark 2:27). Jesus intentionally (consciously) broke the Sabbath laws because any law or rule that is not consciously, deliberately, enacted has no Spirit in it. This makes it an idol that needs to be destroyed, and those who follow the law blindly idolaters.

It is worth noting, even though it is obvious, that idolatry of this sort is alive and well in most churches on any given Sunday morning – when the Jesus prayer is recited without focused attention, the hymns are sung without conscious awareness, and the sermon was jotted down the night before from something the preacher read that week. Hands are shook at the end of the

---

1 Agneta Sutton, "Teilhard de Chardin's Christocentric Trinitarianism" in *New Black Friars* 92, no. 1037 (January 2011): 90–103.

service; niceties are exchanged: "You really gave us something to think about this week." But truly, not much of anything has happened. This performance goes on week after week and the whole community colludes in the charade. Why? Because there has been an unconscious agreement made at the level of ego and personality not to allow Love to shatter the idol that we call worship. The seed within the husk, that is, the word of the kin(g)dom of God, has not landed in fertile soil; the yeast of consciousness has not activated the proceedings. It is an exercise in idolatry, the love of form over substance.

Buried treasure and the pearl of great price

Two other images that Jesus uses to illustrate how we enter or see the kin(g) dom of God highlight this inside-out orientation. The buried treasure and the pearl of great price require a search into a hidden, interior dimension, where we'll discover the real treasure. To get to the pearl, the diver first needs to descend to the bottom of the sea to retrieve the oyster. This in itself requires much training of the lungs and involves serious risk to the divers. (It reminds me of initiation rituals or ordeals in tribal cultures, which are used to consciously catalyze the transition from childhood to adulthood, the evolutionary development of the participant.) Then the shell of the oyster must be cracked open. Only after this interior quest to the depths and the act of prying open the shell does the seeker find what he or she has been looking for.

The good news, from an evolutionary point of view, is that there is a natural evolutionary drive that carries us toward the treasure we seek, if we will but align ourselves with it and consciously remove all obstacles (idols) in our pursuit. This requires conscious attention to our own lives as a wisdom teacher. It is why Jesus taught his disciples the importance of being "alert" or "awake." The spiritual journey is about waking up to the depth dimension that is animating us (Spirit); it is about awakening to the obstacles (idols) that keep us asleep and therefore aligned with consensus reality versus the kin(g)dom of God. When we are alert to the ordinary details of our life as the theatre of Spirit, the inner and the outer are united, issuing in a life of abundance, gratitude, and self-donation to the ongoing evolution of the universe.

There is an evolutionary grace that is hard-wired into the cosmos, which one can feel as the creative principle itself (the Logos or Word). This is the seed that was sown in the material universe and eventuated, after 13.8 billion years of evolution, as our lives. The life within the seed can either flourish or wither, and this largely depends, as I've said, upon our willingness to awaken to the Word (the creative impulse) that is manifesting *in* us, *through* us, and *as* us. To awaken to the realization that we are the presence of the Word (Logos, Wisdom, Creative Principle) in human form is to realize, with Jesus of Nazareth, our sacred purpose and vocation – to participate in the creation of the future of Love.

This is the sacred depth dimension of our lives. We are the personalization of the evolutionary impulse, and we are being allured, non-coercively, to participate in the completion or the perfection of Love. This is our mystic identity with the Word, with this creative impulse. It is hidden, or buried, within the evolutionary current itself, and our spiritual quest is animated by it.

We also feel an allurement from the unrealized future that needs us in order to be realized. As mentioned in an earlier chapter, Teilhard de Chardin called this the Omega Point. Or you could call it the Cosmic Christ, or the eternal Word, the alpha and omega, the beginning and the end.

As already noted, the Cosmic Christ is not up above, but up ahead. S/he is the future, not as tomorrow or ten years down the road, but rather the future as our highest possibility waiting to be realized through our participation. To the extent that we are living out of our highest potential, we are living that future *now*.

As the angel at the tomb of Jesus put it in Matthew's gospel, "Do not be afraid; I know that you are looking for Jesus who was crucified. He is not here; for he has been raised, as he said. Come, see the place where he lay. Then go quickly and tell his disciples, 'He has been raised from the dead, and indeed he is going ahead of you to Galilee; there you will see him'" (Matthew 28:5–7).

Galilee can be understood as a metaphor describing the better future (held in the heart of the Cosmic Christ), always up ahead, beckoning us to participate in its fulfillment. To feel this allurement is to undergo a transformation from idolatrous desire (for a perpetuation of the very conditions that are enslaving us) to holy longing (to go to Galilee).

This holy longing is the good yeast that is mixed in with, and present as, an evolutionary current for realization. This is the zest that compels us to wake up, grow up, and step up as human beings capable of and indeed responsible for giving shape to that future by surrendering to this evolutionary grace of the Holy Spirit. This is how we enter into the kin(g)dom of God – that condition of full, unrestrained participation in giving shape to a future that will increasingly reflected the Love that is G_d. We are anything but alone in this vocation. Spirit, according to Paul, equips us for this process of *growing up* to realize our full humanity, which is to attain the "stature of Christ." It is where the whole universe is headed.

> And he gave the apostles, the prophets, the evangelists, the shepherds and teachers, to equip the saints for the work of ministry, for building up the body of Christ, until we all attain to the unity of the faith and of the knowledge of the Son of God, to mature humanness, to the measure of the stature of the fullness of Christ, *so that we may no longer be children…* (Ephesians 4:11–14a, *English Standard Version*).

EIGHT

The Churchless Incarnation

Faith itself sometimes needs to be stripped of its social and historical encrustations and returned to its first, churchless incarnation in the human heart.
— Christian Wiman, poet, philosopher

Whenever a spiritual movement gets more than a handful of followers, it is going to have to get organized. There will be agreements made, conscious or unconscious, rules to observe, boundaries set, the emergence of leaders (and with this, power politics). Questions will be raised and somehow answers about who's in and who's out, and how to discern this, will be agreed upon; as will codes of conduct (how to behave), how to support and resource the community, and whether it will actively seek new followers. And there will be more questions and answers put forward: How often, in what ways, and for what purpose will the group gather? What are the core beliefs and values of the group? How will the group discipline its members, or will it?

By the time a community of spiritual seekers has answered these questions, a culture and a structure has formed. This is what poet Christian Wiman calls "the historical and cultural encrustations" of faith. This is what he suggests needs to be stripped down in order to return to the "churchless incarnation of the heart."

He's right, I think, and it needs to be understood that his ideal faith, rooted in the heart, necessarily goes through these periods of encrustation along with a stripping process. In truth, the truly alive human being goes through this stripping process many times in relation to his own personality.

The challenge for institutional incarnation is that there are many individuals in the community who do not feel the same way. Those holding power, whose careers depend on the encrustation; those who use the institutional rituals as a bulwark precisely against the stripping and renewing, are often deeply attached to the status quo.

Once-born and twice-born churchgoers

Roughly speaking, there are two kinds of people in the church that I've experienced. The first type looks at the human condition and their own lot in life and by and large concludes that life is pretty good. What is required is a minor weekly tweaking of conditions: a good "message" on Sunday morning, something more along the lines of a reminder to be good citizens. These are the ones who bring their children to church to "expose" them to Christian values so that "one day, they will be able to make their own decision." The church is the Good Ship Morality in a sea of cultural turbulence and sin – thank G_d they are aboard. Their moral and spiritual obligation is to offer a life preserver to those in need. These folk aren't really interested in change. Even many so-called liberals can have an understanding of the church that is quite nostalgic. They want church to be the way they remember it.

Then there are those who know what it's like to be drowning. You could call this type "twice-born humans." This doesn't necessarily mean that they are fundamentalists in their orientation. They know the power of self-deception. They have been, with Jesus, to the wilderness, where they have been tempted by the demons of sex, status, security, and sustenance. They know how easy it is to confuse the contracted self with their true nature, and they know how addicted they are to their contracted self. They understand that stripping of the encrusted self is precisely what is required and it's why they've come to church. They have tasted Spirit, both as the power that drove them, with Jesus, into the wilderness in the first place, and then led them to the church. These folk have come precisely to be stripped down, to die to their former self and their former life, and to be born again, a new creation.

The church that is explicitly evolutionary consists primarily of the twice-born kind of person. In truth, a congregation of evolving mystics may undergo multiple spiritual births, individually, culturally, and in how it is organized.

The story of Nicodemus, a Pharisee, with Jesus, as told in John's gospel, reflects a man of the first type flirting with becoming the second type. What follows is a midrash I wrote about the encounter, and posted on my website, Home for Evolving Mystics (www.brucesanguin.com).

A terrible freedom: the story of Nicodemus

Nicodemus lay in bed before sunrise, awakened by wind, thinking about his visit with the Nazarene last night, a visit he had no business making, even under cover of night, with his head covered so he wouldn't be spotted by the other doctors of religion. They too, he knew, were fascinated by the peasant from north of nowhere. But they had dismissed him. A quack, a charlatan, another messianic pretender. How could they, he asked himself, dismiss the healings, the flow of wisdom, the spiritual authority of his teachings?

He knew why already. He broke laws, he challenged tradition, and he had a knowing that was not hearsay. Most of all he showed little respect for their office, their status among the people. He saw into their souls and this, above all, they could not tolerate. They wouldn't hear him because they couldn't hear him without going through the turmoil Nicodemus was undergoing.

Nicodemus saw the wind move the curtain beside the bed, listened to the breathing of his beloved sleeping wife. How did the Nazarene put it? "The wind blows where it chooses, and you hear the sound of it, but you do not know where it comes from or where it goes. So it is with everyone who is born of the Spirit."

A longing surged inside Nicodemus. He remembered his youth when he would run through the wheat fields with the local dogs trailing behind him. He would lie on his back with the dogs licking his face, and wonder at what must lie beyond the blue dome. He wanted it all. He felt life with an immediacy that made him feel like he was going to explode. Yes, it was freedom he longed for. The freedom to follow the wind wherever it blows. The freedom to remain curious and not know. The freedom to follow a hunch, to stake your life on it.

This Nazarene moved like the wind. He was nobody's slave, but everybody's servant. He never seemed to need to think about what he was going to say before he said it. And when he spoke, it was like thunder. His voice was the promise of a great relief coming soon, like the spring rains. When it was time to move on, he moved on. When it was time to stop, he stopped. Nothing seemed to be in the way of his listening for the promptings of Spirit. What does he know that I don't? From whence this freedom? How did he never lose it? The wind was not always gentle though, was it, he mused. It "breaks the cedars, the cedars of Lebanon, and strips the forests bare. It causes oaks to whirl."

He had just sung this psalm in the synagogue. We sing these words, he realized, but we don't hear them, or they would tear us up by the roots.

Who could he talk to about all he was going through? But there was nobody who could really hear him, who wouldn't just try to settle him down. Now he knew why he risked everything to talk to the peasant mystic. He felt a moment of shame that he had framed the whole thing as a theological debate, when really what he had wanted to ask was, "Who are you? How do you live like you do? From whence comes your power and wisdom? How is it that you seem so free? What do you see? Why can't I see it? What must I do to see like this?"

How had Jesus put it? "Unless you are born from above, nobody can see the kin(g)dom of God."

This being "born from above" had something to do with letting go of everything that everybody else thought was important. It meant letting go of his carefully constructed beliefs, and of the theological acumen for which he was known and honoured. *Oy vey*, it meant more than this! A moment of terror seized him, when the thought came: "Being born from above means first and foremost letting go of Nicodemus – let go of 'Nicodemus' and everything else will come to you." The mantra repeated itself over and over again. The bed felt like it was spinning. Was he losing his mind?

What is born of the flesh is flesh, and what is born of the Spirit is spirit.

The words were a torment, a torrent that was sweeping him away. Everything he associated with "Nicodemus" he understood was "born of the flesh."

Whatever else Jesus was doing, he was reaching into his soul for the Nicodemus of the wheat fields, for the "him" that was born of the Spirit. It was excruciating, this truth that he knew but did not have the courage to live.

He reviewed his life, a life he had come to love. Too much maybe? A good life by anybody's standards. But at what point did the good become the enemy of the better? Recently he had grown restless. His wife was beginning to worry about him. He had grown impatient with the endless theological debates. What once fascinated him, now just hurt his head. The prayers seemed empty. The rituals seemed to be more of a safeguard against God than a way to connect. He would stare off blankly until his wife called him back.

Maybe his restlessness was a sign that Spirit was blowing him off centre? Maybe *he* was the cedar of Lebanon in need of being broken and stripped bare by the fierce mercy of the wind. He was the mighty oak who wanted, in his soul at least, to be picked up and whirled out of his mind and into submission, by a force stronger than his fear of movement. He hated these thoughts. But he felt alive. He could not deny it.

By the time breakfast was finished, he knew he would forget these thoughts. A necessary amnesia. He knew this because it had been going on every morning for the past couple of years – ever since he caught wind of Jesus. He knew that his wife would make breakfast and serve him. She would tousle his hair as she walked by, and his children would be running around the house. He would leave to gather with his minion for morning prayers. His prayers would help to calm the storm. He would look around at his friends who had celebrated and supported him over the years, and he would reassure himself that this was his life.

He did not understand the tears now streaming down his face as these reassuring thoughts came to him. Or why he got up quietly to close all the windows. It seemed now preposterous to him that after his campfire meeting with Jesus he had thought for just a minute that all things were possible, that he could persuade his wife to follow him, this nomad of the north. He had felt free. God, he had felt free. For just a moment, he had felt the wind at his back.

He wiped the tears away before his wife could see.

This biblical story, likely written over 100 years after Jesus' death, reflects a community that was not yet encrusted. It was a church committed to living by the Spirit. You will know by now that a directly accessible experience of Spirit is this impulse to evolve, which means being born again, and again. In this story, Jesus says that we cannot see the kin(g)dom of G_d unless we are "born from above." Being born from above means being born of the Spirit. And the experience of Spirit for Jesus is analogous to the wind. It blows where it wishes. You hear the sound of the wind, but you don't know where it comes from or where it's going. And the real kicker is what follows: "So it is with everyone who is born of the Spirit."

The nomadic nature of G_d

I come back here to the nomadic image of G_d, and to the image of Jesus himself as nomadic. The nomad is on the move. Pierre Teilhard de Chardin captures how radical the notion of evolution was when it first broke onto the theological scene after Darwin, in the way it implied that movement is descriptive of reality itself. There is both the willingness to move and to be moved, with the understanding that this is just the nature of reality.

> The conflict dates from the day when one man, flying in the face appearance, perceived that the forces of nature are no more unalterably fixed in their orbits than the stars themselves, but that their serene arrangements around us depict the flow of a tremendous tide – the day on which a first voice rang out, crying to Mankind peacefully slumbering in the raft of Earth, "We are moving! We are going forward!...
>
> It is a pleasant and dramatic spectacle, that of Mankind divided to its very depths into two irrevocably opposed camps – one looking toward the horizon and proclaiming, with all its newfound faith, "We are moving", and the other, without shifting its position, obstinately maintaining, "Nothing changes. We are not moving at all![1]

---

1 Pierre Teilhard de Chardin, *The Future of Mankind* (New York: Image Books, 2004), 1.

Teilhard calls those who refuse to see a world in motion – call it the nomadic vision given us by evolution – the "immobilists."

When we examine the deep-time view of evolutionary history, one thing becomes unmistakable. We are citizens of a universe that is on the move. Using the Mount Wilson telescope in southern California, Edwin Hubble (after whom the Hubble space telescope is named) discovered that the farther away a galaxy is from Earth, the faster it moves away. This discovery provided actual proof of Einstein's theory that the universe is expanding out in all directions, creating space and time as it goes. The biological evolution of life on Earth is the narrative of life being lived by a restlessness that is never content, apparently, with a particular form, or in the human realm, with a particular form of consciousness or culture. This process is continually renewing, transforming, being "born again."

Rumi, the 12th-century Sufi poet, captures the mystic appreciation of how being born again is simply a natural expression of the evolutionary trajectory:

I died as mineral and became a plant,

I died as plant and rose to animal,

I died as animal and I was human,

Why should I fear? When was I less by dying?

Yet once more I shall die human,

To soar with angels blessed above.

And when I sacrifice my angel soul

I shall become what no mind ever conceived.

As a human, I will die once more,

Reborn, I will with the angels soar…[2]

The competency of being and becoming

When contemporary mystic Thomas Hubl writes that there are two core competencies for being human – the competency of being and the competency of becoming – what he means by the latter is that we cultivate the capacity to

2 William C. Chittick, *The Sufi Path of Love: The Spiritual Teachings of Rumi* (Albany: New York Press, 1983).

participate consciously in what the universe is already doing. That is, we are being lived by a current of becoming. As I've already discussed, if we refuse to move with this current, we actually make ourselves sick, because we become obstacles to the flow. If this energy is not flowing through us, if our bodies, minds, and spirits have become "encrustations" rather than channels or vessels of this cosmic movement that pervades us, illness follows. In truth, you *are* this process, which has manifested in the form of you. The competency of becoming begins with this awareness, and continues when we consciously align with it. To know this is to be an evolving mystic.

In communities of faith, this illness manifests as stagnation, like a stream that has been dammed. The truth is that if you are not being born again, you are dying. And a dying congregation smells like it. There is a dead feeling. Nothing cooking. Going nowhere in particular. Going through the motions.

In my midrash above, this describes Nicodemus. He had begun to stagnate. Jesus acted as evolutionary provocateur, and unless Nicodemus lets the Spirit blow through his life, unless he *makes a move*, and a radical one at that, death will have its way. His tears, upon closing the window against the breeze, signify his grief in knowing that he is not ready to become a child of the wind. He needs to find a way to live with himself as an immobilist. It's a fundamental decision for communities of faith.

This process of encrustation doesn't take long to set in. It started happening almost immediately after Jesus died and stories of his resurrection began to circulate. We can say with some certainty that Jerusalem, where Peter and Jesus' brother James seemed to be in charge, was a more conservative bunch of disciples, who saw themselves still functioning as practicing Jews – albeit Jews who believed that the Messiah had come in Jesus. They were more for tweaking a few things here and there. Even in the gospel accounts, the editorial additions of the writers of the gospels reveal how difficult it is to follow the Holy Spirit.

Paul was more radical. It put him in tension with the Jerusalem church almost immediately. It didn't help that he was persecuting the church before he underwent his own *metanoia*. He never met Jesus, except after his death in some sort of vision, but my contention is that he caught the spirit of the Christ, working through Jesus, more closely than the Jerusalem gathering. He got that everything had changed, including his religion. Most importantly, he realized that he himself was being lived by the same power that animated Jesus – the Christ. Paul's vision of spiritual community is decidedly stripped down.

The spiritual community that is explicitly evolutionary consists primarily of this kind of person. As I've said, a community of evolving mystics may undergo multiple spiritual births (and deaths) individually, culturally, and in how it is organized. The community comes together for this very purpose.

The spiritual community that understands itself as explicitly evolutionary puts the evolution of souls first. Teilhard puts it this way: the Christian vocation is "no longer merely to ease the suffering, to bind up the wounds or to succor the weak, but through every form of effort and discovery, to urge its powers by love right up to their higher term."[3]

Remember, Teilhard was a priest and a very loving human being. He served as a stretcher-bearer in WWI on the front lines in France. He knew firsthand what it meant to ease suffering, bind up wounds, and provide succour to the weak. But in and through it all, the larger context of the vocation he was called to as one who embraced evolution itself as the activity of the Christ was "through every form of effort and discovery, to urge its powers by love right up to their higher term."

I believe that it's time for a few congregations to emerge that risk making this their primary mandate. Even pastoral care and social justice would be animated by this core directive, which Paul called "pressing on": "I press on toward the goal for the prize of the upward call of God in Christ Jesus" (Philippians 3:14, *English Standard Version*).

This "upward call of God in Christ Jesus" is, in my opinion, Paul's intuitive understanding that we are meant to aspire to the transcendent, twice-born Human. This is what he meant by being "in Christ," with Christ being the loving pull exerted by the Christ who is the perfection of Love awaiting

---

3 Pierre Teilhard de Chardin, *Christianity and Evolution*, trans. Rene Hague (New York: Harcourt, Brace, Jovanovich, 1978), 185.

fulfillment in us.

In my book *The Emerging Church* (second edition), I outline eight "core agreements" that an evolutionary congregation would enter into in order to create a culture of creative emergence. In the next chapter, I will outline the foundations of an evolutionary practice for a spiritual community that is serious about this "upward call of G_d."

—— NINE ——

Practices of Evolutionary Mysticism

God is not the finite, definable God of the theologians who put a ready-made man into a pre-fabricated world. He (sic) is rather that force which strives from a dark original cause toward revelation, that is, toward his (sic) own realization and corporealization. He (sic) manifests himself gradually in the development of life in its various stages.
— Fredrich Christoph Oetinger (1702–1782)

I confess I am somewhat reluctant to include a separate chapter on spiritual practices. My reluctance stems from an understanding that our lives *are* our spiritual practice. We are each here to evolve, and our best and most immediate teacher is our *own* life. Our lives are wisdom teachers. Each and every experience, properly held in consciousness, is a catalyst for us to deepen into the mystery of life, and to take our next step along our evolving soul path.

This flies in the face of the contemporary assumption that our *real* lives have to do with making a living and earning enough to one day retire so that, hopefully, we can leave some kind of legacy for our children. With whatever time and energy is left over, we do our spiritual practice.

When this allegiance to consensus reality is unconscious, the addition of spiritual practices can serve to merely support the illusion. This is, in part, what Karl Marx meant when he said that religion is the "opiate of the masses." "Spirituality" then becomes an addendum to that agenda, not only entrenching the class system politically, but entrenching the personality or the social self on a personal level. Spiritual practice becomes something we do around the edges when we have time.

With the proviso that our practices should in no way be separate from the lives we lead, I've included a number of practices that can support us on an evolving soul-path.

Kenosis

The good news is that the Spirit-infused evolutionary current is always already "on," which means that the most essential practice is getting out of the way of it. Within the Jesus lineage, this is called *kenotic* practice. *Kenosis* is a Greek word that means "emptying." The idea of a *kenotic* practice is derived from the earliest Christian hymn we know in Paul's letter to the Philippians: "Let the same mind be in you that was in Christ Jesus, who, though he was in the form of God, did not regard equality with God as something to be exploited, but *emptied himself...*" (Philippians 2:5–6).

I was tempted to call this chapter "The Great Purge." The practice of what was once called "purgation" informs all traditions, something the Jesus lineage has always recognized. It sounds gruesome, but really it's just a way of talking about *kenosis*. We are being invited, in every moment of every day of our lives, to purge everything in us that is not love. If you are like me, that's a fairly long list. It begins with the purging of the trauma around which our ego or small self has been constructed as compensation for a pain too great to endure.

What pain? We all arrived here expecting to be loved unconditionally, to be recognized for the gift that we are, to be drawn into fullness of being by our mother's making space for our intrinsic radiance to shine – and after infancy and toddlerhood, for schools, friends, and employers to do the same. When this does not happen, for whatever reasons, it is a shock to our system, a trauma. And when any physical or sexual abuse is added to this unresponsive environment, the trauma only deepens. It goes deep within our unconscious and rules our life from outside of conscious awareness. For our entire life, we can live with our lives being run unconsciously by our traumatized personality. We can even become experts in our field and have what looks to others like a "normal" life.

But one day, if we are lucky, we awaken to realize that our life has not been our own. We have not been living from soul. And when our soul finally comes on line, guess what? We discover our essential nature, which is love itself. The way we know this initially is that we feel such enormous love for the little person inside of us that was not loved.

We talk a lot about self-love, but in my case I always tried to love myself from my ego. But it's not the ego's job to love. It's the ego's job to survive, and we can be grateful for the ingenuity and creativity the ego displays in doing this. But it's not until we come back in touch with our essential nature, or soul, that we are able to authentically love self, and importantly, love those who hurt us.

This is why the core practice has to do with purging, or self-emptying. What we empty ourselves of is essentially the compensated self. This takes time. Usually we need professional help.

This insight around purging came to me as I was physically purging (vomiting) during an *Ayahuasca* ceremony. It was a direct teaching during which my own early trauma was shown to me graphically. Once the trauma was brought to the light of conscious awareness, I experienced an immense love and compassion toward myself and my perpetrator. The effectiveness of psychoactive (entheogens) substances when used ceremonially and in the context of therapy is now very well researched and documented. In my case, the ceremony acted as a spiritual catalyst as well.

The bad news is that this self-emptying isn't easy. In fact, we shaped our personalities (our social self) so that we could be full of ourselves, so to speak. We tend to want to hold on, rather than let go. The project of establishing ourselves as a "somebody" in the world is critical to getting on in the world. The problem is that most of us suspect, for any number of reasons, that if you scratch the surface, we are nobodies. We carry wounds within us that we compensated for, necessarily, by trying as best we could to prop up our fragile selves.

Somehow, we need to find the "mind" of the Christ (our soul is connected to this presence), which knows itself to be deeply loved, has nothing to prove, nothing to compensate for, and has no need to either prop itself up with false posturing, or collapse in helplessness and victimhood. To have the mind of Christ, on this psychological and emotional level, is to be in the world as a sovereign self, orienting from deep self-acceptance, able to stay connected across differences, and be self-defined. (I am "this" and not "that." I value "this," but not "that." This is where I take my stand). To have the "mind of Christ" on a spiritual level means awakening to our true nature as an expression of the nature of Reality. In theological terms, it means awakening to the *imago Dei* (image of G_d) that is always present, yet often buried beneath layers of personality. The *imago Dei* is unconditional love.

The goal of the practices can be variously understood. Many of them are about overcoming the illusion of separation: death from life; body from mind and spirit; human from Earth and Cosmos. Modernity brought us many wonderful medical and technological advances, but the costs were also high, none more so than the felt sense that humans are separate from the rest of existence. It is fair to say that our psyches, as well as our economic, political, religious and social systems are reflections of this separation. The costs to our planet and to our sense of well-being are now well-documented. The mystic's knowledge of the condition of no-separation alone has the power to elevate the human being and our planet out of our current condition of alienation.

The universe had been constructing itself with staggering perfection long before we ever came on the scene. This flow of ever-emergent creativity left galaxies, solar systems, living planets, and human beings in its wake. Much spiritual practice is about learning to trust that we are living artifacts of this flow of life, and that what it wants to do through us is to bring new and improved futures into existence. It has been revealed to me that the whole universe is participating in drawing forth from us everything that is not love. When we are actively purging or emptying, the flow of life, which is evolving us toward the perfection of love, takes over.

This means we are involved in a staggering mystery. And the practice requires deep and consistent contemplation of the deeply felt sense that our lives are being lived by this mystery. Let me say it again. Much spiritual practice is simply, but profoundly, about trusting that this process is making of our lives an honourable contribution to the evolving mystery of love. This requires a life of surrender.

And yet, paradoxically, the universe has created the human being as a conscious centre of this evolutionary creativity. Therefore, we are responsible, as free creator/creatures, to use this freedom and this creativity to participate in the emergence of a future that is more beautiful, good, and true. In other words, trusting that this process is living us does not mean abdicating our responsibility as co-creators. It takes a lifetime to strike the balance between "allowing" and taking action. Allowing simply means taking reality as it is and not fighting with it. Then, it is a matter of trusting that the same power out of which galaxies emerged continues to work, in all circumstances, "good" or "bad," in our lives. Once we have learned radical acceptance of reality, then we engage our creative capacities and our personal will to act decisively for the "future our hearts know is possible."[1]

The practices that follow are loosely related to my eight Core Agreements for an Evolving Culture.[2]

Core Agreements 1 and 2:
Listen for Emergence
Speak True Words

Listening and speaking true words (evolving the "We")

At the most basic level, we can neither listen nor speak true words when we are coming from a condition of fear. When this is the case, we will always speak the pleasing word, not our deepest truth. Similarly, we literally cannot hear what is being said if we chronically interpret what is being said to us as confirming a negative self-image we have of ourselves. Whether speaking or listening, when we are contracted in fear, the conversation will always end up being about "me." This may seem obvious, but it needs to be said that in the

---

1 *The Surrender Experiment* by Michael A. Singer is an inspiring story of a man who lived his whole life by this practice.

2 Thanks to Craig Hamilton for inspiring these agreements.

life of the community, if individuals are not able to distinguish between their compensated, fear-based self, and their authentic self, these core agreements will never get off the ground. This speaks to the importance of shadow work in the context of therapy, which is discussed under the agreement "Take Responsibility."

I would like to focus on one particular practice in the context of this first agreement. The leading edge of evolutionary spirituality is occurring in the "we-space." A we-space is a way of being together with the conscious intention to create a space in which a future (the highest possibility now) emerges out of a gathering of sovereign individuals. A "we space" is unique to each particular group, and transcends (but includes) the personalities and intelligence of any of the individual participants.

"Where two or three are gathered in my name, there am I in the midst."

We have defined the Christ as the principle of creative transformation, personalized in Jesus and in other humans as love. This teaching doesn't deny that the Christ is available to individuals, but the focus here is on what kind of wisdom emerges in the collective ("two or three" minimally), when the intention is to open to the mind and heart of the Christ.

Christ emerges in the space between the individuals—the "we space".

The practice requires that each person in the group empty (*kenosis*) of their contracted or small self so that, as much as possible, s/he is available to attune to the new future, the new conversation, the new wisdom, that wants to emerge. S/he must set aside all personal agendas – for example, displaying how much s/he knows about a subject, all past narratives on a theme, or one's own unmet social needs (the need to belong, for status, for security, etc.). These agendas will be there for the individual to return to. It's not like they will disappear. But they are suspended for the duration of the practice.

I've been part of groups practicing we-space when someone has spoken from the small self. It is immediately obvious when someone is trying to meet an underlying personal agenda (even when it is *apparently* on theme). It is as though something non-resonant with the deeper wisdom that wants to emerge has entered the space, and it always drops with a thud to the ground.

The practice itself, below, is one I learned in a group led by Miriam and Stephan Martineau. They have graciously allowed me to reprint this. Miriam and Stephan are brilliant teachers and practitioners of we-space. I should also mentioned that Dr. Olen Gunnlaugson, associate professor of Business Administration at Laval University, Canada, is doing groundbreaking research into this practice.

The practice

- Gather in a quiet space, in circle formation, no distractions, bringing elements from earth to the center, and lighting a candle.
- Read the following questions out loud to remind each participant that we are about to listen and speak from Source:
- Is now the time? Is this the space? Am I the one? Is it from God?
- Open eyes / Sit up straight / Show up fully.
- Ring bells: three times to start.
- Devotional prayer.
- Guidance: Ground of Being (in which the group is helped to connect to Source).
- Inspirational reading of a text. (This could be a poem, a scriptural text, or an inspirational quote.)
- Read these invocations and invitations out loud:
  1. May we surrender into witnessing, allowing Presence to deepen.
  2. May we suspend the "known," being open and curious.
  3. May we listen deeply to what wants to emerge, building on the truth of what has been said.
  4. May we engage passionately, infusing the space with life energy and expectancy.
  5. May we be mindful of self, especially our inner faculty of discernment.
  6. May we be mindful of other, attuning to the thread of truth.
  7. May we be mindful of the space, informed by the whole field.

Share whatever comes to you in response to the inspirational reading. Dive in fully, as awake as possible, into the emergent co-created unfolding!

Zen counting

- Put people in groups and form a circle.
- The goal is to count to 10 or 15. (The larger the group the lower the number.)
- Eyes closed, only one person can say the number at a time, if two or more people say the number at the same time, start over at one.

You will find with this exercise that people will be required to listen deeply, but as much to the spaces between the sounds as to the actual sound of the number being spoken. They will also be required to tune into an *interior* clue as to when it is their moment to say a number. They will need to use their intuition and only speak when they feel inwardly compelled to speak. This practice works really well for learning to speak and listen as a "We."

Core Agreement 3:
Exemplify the Adventure of Becoming

Transform desire into holy longings

As those who are committed to the conscious evolution of love, we are expected to reflect this path in how we live, how we relate, and in all of our actions. In a previous age of traditional religious consciousness, this primarily meant obeying the laws of an external G_d and "His" representatives in the church or temple. While living with high ethical standards is included in the enactment of this agreement, the fundamental commitment is to remove all obstacles to loving more deeply, letting nothing impede the impulse for self-transcendence for the sake of love.

If we are to be exemplars of evolutionary mysticism, our lives need to be witnesses first and foremost to the unswerving commitment to evolve. We will be seen as people who are willing to risk everything in dedication to the evolution of consciousness, culture, and our social systems. In traditional Christian language, this is what it means to "follow Christ." This doesn't mean following in Jesus' footsteps, as noble as that ideal might be. It means being animated by the same power (the power of creative transformation – Christ – expressed as love) that animated him, and letting nothing get in the way of this.

Recognizing that we live in an age of multiple addictions, a core practice of this agreement is to grow in our capacity to transform our egoic desires (for more of what we already have) into *holy longings*.

In this exercise, we will assume that a primary obstacle to allowing love to have its way with us is a desire that results in addiction. Desire is any craving for more of what you know by any rational standard you've had enough of, or is not good for you, your family, your human or Earth community. Desires are urgent (but not important), unhealthy, short-term, and insatiable. Longings are important (but not urgent), health-creating, long-term, and soul-satisfying.

The practice

- The moment you become aware of an unhealthy desire, don't fight with it. As with the mantra meditation (below), simply let it be in your awareness, and then let it be a signal that you have right at this moment an opportunity to get in touch with a holy or a noble longing.
- In your mind, focus on the deeper longing. Try to connect the longing in some way with the craving.
- Think of one small action you can do to honour the longing. This is not the same as satisfying the longing. Remember that longing is a core pleasure for the soul, reminding us of the sacredness of life, and drawing us back to our evolutionary path.
- Express gratitude for the desire that gave you the opportunity to return to your longing, and for the longing that is the presence of Spirit, praying through you.

Example

I'm out shopping. I have just eaten lunch, but I see a lemon tart displayed in the best bakery in town. And then I think how great it would taste with a latte.

I find myself rationalizing that it would be okay, just this once, even though I have already had my quota of caffeine, and because of the start of some arthritis I know that the sugar is an inflammatory.

I let this desire signal to me my deeper longing for two things: first, for greater health and wellbeing in myself and, second, for more public awareness about how excessive caffeine and sugar affect the body long-term, and the impact both of these substances have on our perception and behaviour. I remember how in the past these substances would be used ceremonially. I also think about Dierdre Barrett's book *Supernormal Stimuli*. I decide that I'm going to blog about this and share what happened to me with my readers. I express gratitude for my desire for caffeine and sugar, for reminding me about more public awareness. As I do this, I consider the even larger implications for the food industry and make a mental note to do some more research.

Exercise: Holy longing timeline

On a sheet of paper, divide your life into decades or any number of years. For example, you could use intervals of seven years instead of ten. Identify for each decade what you remember your core longing to be, right up to the present. For example, here's what mine might look like:

0–10: Acceptance and friendship

11–20: To play and master sports

21–30: Knowing *about* G_d, the meaning of life, intellectual learning

31–40: Professional competency/vocational identity, love

41–50: Sharing wisdom, deepening capacity for love, living from soul

51–60: Open new doors of perception, knowing G_d directly, deepening capacity for love

As you can see, there may be more than one longing in each decade. Also, longings may be carried over from one decade to another, as with my desire to know love more deeply.

When you have completed your Longing Timeline, share it with a loved one or a friend. Reflect on how your longings have organized your life. Generally speaking, the more you have honoured your holy longings, the more you satisfied and happy you are. Ask yourself if there are any longings that you have not allowed sufficiently to deepen within you? Identify the reasons for this. What have been the costs of following your longings? What have been the rewards? Can you imagine that Spirit has been in your longings, and that your evolving soul-path has been cleared by these longings? Spend time contemplating this mystery.

Core Agreement 4:
Steward Spaciousness

The practice: meditation

The word translated as "salvation" in the New Testament is derived from the Hebrew root *yesha*, which means spaciousness. Jesus' name is a derivation of this root. He is the one who saves by creating spaciousness. In the Hebrew scriptures, G_d saves by setting the people down in a large space, safe from their enemies. On a personal level, spaciousness as a mode of consciousness can be contrasted with contraction. Whenever we are afraid, anxious, or ashamed we contract into a very small expression of the universe. In this state, we interpret our experience as though the universe was hostile and out to get us. We are hyper-vigilant in our self-protectiveness. We defend ourselves from what we perceive to be a hostile world. It is imperative, if we intend to evolve our spiritual life, that we are able to expand beyond the fortified walls of our personality (which were built in large part to compensate for failures of love), and discover the spaciousness by which we know ourselves to be a beautiful manifestation of Source.

Meditation is one of the most effective practices to help us to be able to observe our fears and anxieties, with a witnessing consciousness, and return to a condition of spaciousness.

Assuming that we're committed to doing shadow work (see below), meditation is an ancient practice for quieting the mind, which works over time because of fear and habit. (Without doing the shadow-work, meditation merely promotes spiritual by-passing.)

There are two main types of meditation. One uses concentration – on a mantra or sacred phrase or an object like a candle – to focus the mind. In the lineage of Jesus, this has become known as centring prayer. Fr. Thomas Keating has dedicated his life to teaching this method.

Instructions using a mantra:

- Ideally, choose two times in the day when you won't be interrupted. If you can't find two times, just start with one period of meditation. Silence the ringer on your phones.
- Choose a simple phrase such as "G_d is love," "You are with me," or "I am the universe."
- Close your eyes and sit in a conscious posture, usually with feet on the ground, and back relatively upright. Set an alarm for 20 minutes.
- Make a conscious intention to "consent to the presence of G_d" in this time.
- Repeat the sacred phrase out loud eight to ten times, and then silently to yourself.
- Continue to repeat the phrase throughout the meditation.
- When you notice thoughts, images, and feelings arising in your mind, simply acknowledge them. They are like clouds floating through your awareness. Let them pass. Let them be signals for you to return to your mantra. That is all they are. Their presence doesn't mean you've failed. In fact, there is no goal here, no place to get to. Whatever is arising is exactly what needs to arise. Don't try to *not* have thoughts. Just return to your sacred phrase, gently. You may notice yourself being carried away by a particular thought. That's okay. When you notice, it is a signal to return to your mantra. There is no struggle. No right and wrong.
- When your meditation is over, open your eyes very gently and slowly. Try not to be in a rush to get to the next thing. It can be pleasurable just taking in objects in the room one at a time.

Instructions without a mantra

In this kind of meditation, you will simply notice your thoughts. The goal is to have no relationship with the thoughts, images, feelings that arise. You simply notice and accept, without any agenda to change, whatever is arising in you. Meditation teacher Andrew Cohen teaches that the simplest instructions for this kind of meditation are: Be still, be at ease, pay attention.[3]

For Cohen, *being still* is a metaphor for freedom. We directly participate in liberating ourselves from the compulsive activity of the contracted self and its mind. When we make a conscious intention to not be moved by these voices that entrap us, we are already experiencing a form of enlightenment.

Being at ease is a metaphor for liberation from a world that would have us believe that we are never safe and that if we stop striving for more there will be disastrous consequences. It is fair to say that the Western, capitalistic ethos normalizes the driven personality. The underlying message is that if we stop controlling reality, something awful will befall us. In meditation, we experience liberation from this vague anxiety that something is deeply wrong with the world and with us. We rest in the perfection, to use a Buddhist metaphor.

For Cohen, *pay attention* is a metaphor for liberation from all thoughts and feelings that emanate from the contracted self. As we cultivate this competency, we become increasingly aware of the "witnessing consciousness" or simply the witness, which is that aspect of us that is always, already aware of everything. The witness is able to see what is arising in meditation, but not identify with it. In this way, what was subjective and invisible (the mind of our contracted self) becomes objective and visible. When this occurs, we have developed an enlightened relationship with our mind.

- Follow all the steps for the mantra meditation, only don't introduce the mantra. Simply witness what is arising. Some forms of meditation recommend naming what arises. For example, when we be-

---

3 Andrew is one of those teachers, who by his own recent admission, neglected to do his shadow work, and as a result hurt many of his students. He has publicly apologized for his behavior with his core students. Referencing him here in no way condones his actions. That said, his articulation of the dynamics of meditation are lucid and helpful.

come aware of a thought, say "thought" to ourselves. When we become aware of a sensation, say "sensation." When we become aware of some bodily discomfort, say "discomfort."

- The practice involves letting all things be the way they are, without feeling the need to change anything. Meditation teacher Jeff Carreira calls his practice of meditation The Practice of No Problems.

Core Agreement 5:
Fail Bravely

The practice: Receive feedback as information

I remember the first time I used GPS. When I made a mistake, a friendly female voice would alert me to my mistake in a very non-judgmental way: "Make a U-turn at your earliest possible convenience." I felt no shame. My male ego wasn't even close to being tweaked. I was being corrected, but in such a way that I was receiving it as objective information about a mistake I had made, not as character assassination. Many of us were made to feel so much shame when we made a mistake as children that we carried this with us into adulthood. Now there is no external authority controlling our behaviour. We don't need one. We have learned to become hyper-vigilant about monitoring ourselves so that we will never need to be corrected and risk feeling ashamed again. We were taught to see mistakes as failure and failure as something to be avoided at all costs.

Someone once said that science is the art of failing again and again, but with each failure coming closer to the truth. Edison failed repeatedly in his attempt to invent the light bulb, but his conclusion was that he simply learned 1,000 ways not to make a light bulb.

A simple practice for "Failing Bravely" is to take up a new activity, like learning a new instrument or writing a poem or a song. Recently I started taking Tango lessons. The instructor is a young guy from Argentina who doesn't believe in practicing "steps." Rather, the dance is an emergent dynamic that arises from deeply attuning to your partner, and making micro-adjustments, according to what you "read" your partner doing. It literally emerges from subtle, energetic shifts. I found myself literally frozen for a long, long time. I simply didn't know where to go with it. I wanted him to show me what it looked like. I wanted to watch a YouTube video. But he let me squirm. I was afraid of failing, of getting it wrong, of taking a wrong step. Despite his repeated attempts to assure me that there is no way to get it wrong, I was paralyzed by fear. Until I let go and made the dance up, in a way, out of our mutual missteps my body was frozen. It would make for a great meditation to spend some time reflecting on how I learned to be so afraid of failure.

But at some point we need to get over it. If we are living our lives playing it safe, as individuals or collectively as institutions, in order to defend ourselves against making a mistake, being wrong, or failing in some way, we are placing barriers in the way of our evolution.

Exercise

- Approach a trusted friend or a spouse with the intention of asking them for direct feedback about how they are experiencing you.
- Assume that this person is your friend and ally in your evolving journey.
- Make a decision that you will not defend yourself.
- Write down all that this person tells you, like you are reporting about somebody else. With the mindset of a journalist, become very curious about the feedback you are getting.
- Thank this person for their feedback.
- Take this information and go to a quiet place.
- Identify any lingering emotional responses and take responsibility for them.
- You may choose to take these emotional responses to a therapist. (See shadow work below.)

Exercise: Live like you are going to die

As I was writing this book, I turned 60. It wasn't traumatic for me, but it was a wake-up call. The realization I had was that everything I had done in my life up to this point laid the foundations for this final act of my life. I made some very difficult decisions in order to get myself to where I was. These decisions were born of an awareness that I wasn't going to live forever. My mortality was front and centre, but not in a morbid way. It was a quickening. Here I am. I have, by some grace, arrived at this turning point with very little preventing me from being "all in." Or to use the passive voice, there was nothing stopping the evolutionary grace that animates the whole cosmos, from lighting me up and leading me into a fuller manifestation of "love and of life and wings: and of the gay great happening illimitably earth."[4] I know at this point that if I am in the way of this, I am 100% committed to discovering the obstacle that I am placing in my soul's path, and allowing it to be removed.

Another name for this agreement is what evolutionary spirituality teacher Craig Hamilton calls "risk everything." For the sake of the evolution of your soul, your community, and of society, risk everything that is not aligned with your deepest intuition of why you are here. This is at the heart of the gospel message. Jesus calls the disciples and they leave everything to follow him. As mentioned in a previous chapter, I don't believe that this was hyperbole. I believe that Jesus' transparency to his own soul and to Spirit directly connected to the souls of his followers. His clarity of purpose and his expansive love reminded them of why they arrived in the first place. Jesus removed obstacles.

More conservative Christians talk about "Jesus dying for our sins." That's not how I would put it. Rather, Jesus, acting with the powers of a shaman, drew from the world into his own being all that was not love. To be in his presence was to want to participate in the Great Purge. In the story of the resurrection, when the women arrive at the tomb, the stone has been removed. This removal of obstacles is, as I've said, the heart of spiritual practice, the secret of resurrection as a way of life.

What holds many people back from evolving is fear of failure. Our medical system portrays death as the ultimate failure. We are required to fight it,

---

4 From E. E. Cummings, "i thank You God for most this amazing," 1950.

conquer it, and overcome it. Which, when you think about it, is crazy. The best "solution" we've come up with for death, in what Stephen Jenkinson calls "the death trade," is "cope, dope, and hope."[5] But nobody, as the saying goes, gets out of here alive.

Death is not a failure. It is an ending we must face consciously. To "die wise," as Jenkinson puts it, is to live as though we know we are going to die. It is a natural limit that galvanizes our attention, causing us to contemplate how we are living and how we want to live. It requires that we take our life seriously. The evolutionary mystic is not here to transcend death, but to allow mortality to be an evolutionary provocation to live with more intensity, intimacy, immensity, and intentionality. Jesus' disciples refused to accept that Jesus himself was going to suffer and die. Jesus takes Peter's denial of death as a trick of the Satan, the one opposed to the divine ways.

The reality that life comes to an end makes being alive all the more precious. To love someone with an open heart is to realize that your heart is going to be broken one day, which makes the love even sweeter. To contemplate death is to feel life more deeply. I remember being with my beloved in a movie theatre with her head resting on my shoulder. I felt the warmth of her head through my shirt, and knew it to be the warmth of life itself that was pulsing against my skin. This being alive, it struck me, is a profound mystery and a profound gift. Life is all around us, everywhere, throbbing, moving, flying, crawling, resting, growing, making flowers. All of it is animated by a life force that is both irrepressible and that seems to pour itself out into the world purposively. And then I started to cry. This beauty would end. Death intensifies our awareness of life. If we have the courage, we fall in love with it, we praise it, we express gratitude.

To fail bravely when it comes to dying is to keep our hearts open as we say good-bye to it all, to our loved ones, and to a world that has supported us. We keep our hearts open despite knowing that we are all going to "fail" when it comes to death. This will make it a magnificent defeat, an ultimate defeat

---

5 Stephen Jenkinson, Die Wise: A Manifesto for Sanity and Soul (North Atlantic Books, 2015).

that offers a gift, *if* we allow it to inspire us to cherish every moment, every exchange of love, every drop of rain and ray of light. This defeat will be a gift if we allow it to keep us alert to the question and process of discerning the work we have left to do.

Exercise: Imagining your death

- Begin by closing your eyes and imagining your dying time.
- Where are you?
- Notice the room you are in. If you are outside, notice the surroundings.
- Who is with you?
- How do you feel?
- What are you doing?
- What matters most?
- You have been asked to write your own epitaph. In one or two sentences, describe your life.
- People are saying good-bye to you. What are they saying about you?
- Are you aware of any regrets as you prepare to die?
- Do you have any unfinished business left to do?
- Imagine now that you have died.
- What is it that your soul most longs for from those you have left?
- What do you most miss?
- Slowly begin to open your eyes.

Journalling

Record your experience in a journal. Think of the time you have left, today, tomorrow, and who knows how long? What calls to you? Is there anything in your life that you want to change? Are there any obstacles standing between you and your ability to experience life more deeply that you are open to having removed? Are there any limiting beliefs that are keeping you from realizing your full potential? Are there any dreams that you've always had but were afraid to pursue for fear of failure?

Core Agreement 6:
Face Crisis as Opportunity

In the evolution of the universe, there were many potential show-stoppers, such as the death of stars (supernovae), the oxygen crisis (when oxygen was a poisonous gas), ice ages, and five ages of extinction. This is a very short list of the various crises the universe faced. In each case, inherent resiliency (call it the fierce force of life) prevailed. The key to this resiliency in the face of crisis was that the seeds of the new intelligences required to meet and transcend the crisis were inherent in the crisis itself.

This is what leads futurist Barbara Marx Hubbard to conclude that the "crisis is the birth." Our species is facing crises on multiple fronts: overpopulation, global warming, soil erosion, toxic poisoning of the air and soil, rising sea levels, etc. These are only the physical threats. We are also undergoing a significant spiritual crisis. Never before in the history of civilization have we been so spiritually dead as a collective. Philosophical materialism and its proponents are very effectively persuading the next generation that there is no purpose and ultimately no meaning in the universe, except that which we arbitrarily construct. Spiritual ignorance is at an all-time high.

Yet all religious traditions have a place for spiritual ignorance as the necessary precursor of awakening. The deeper the ignorance, the more profound the potential awakening. Embedded in these physical and spiritual crises are the latent intelligences that will be required to overcome them. The crises can be held as the provocateur of the new thing that will come in their wake, the new Earth and the New Human.

The practice

This practice is more of a comprehensive attitude toward global, spiritual, and personal crises. It has been said that "evolutionaries" are intrinsically hopeful. But this shouldn't be a "Pollyannaish" optimism. Rather, when we adopt the "big history" perspective, we realize that this irrepressible life force, this creativity, has yet to be thwarted and it is highly unlikely (and I mean this evidentially) that this creativity will stop creating, even if we refuse to wake up. Call it Spirit or life force, it is eternal, it is relentless, and it is intent on creating a world of beauty, truth, and goodness.

On a more personal level, this agreement and practice requires that we hold our own life experience as a wisdom teacher. We ask ourselves, in the face of crisis, what is the teaching in this for me? How am I being called to wake up, grow up, and step up? What is the opportunity in the crisis that is facing me? When we face these kinds of crises there is a tendency to either collapse or prop ourselves up artificially. We adopt these stances because we learned in our families of origin that we were powerless to negotiate a new future. This is why shadow work is so important. We need to bring this felt sense of powerlessness to the light of consciousness and ask whether it is actually true? What would life be like for us if it wasn't true? Can you name two or three times in your life when you displayed genuine resiliency? If you can't, ask a friend to help you. You'll discover that there have been plenty of times.

And remember, resilience is not foreign to you. You are the evolving universe in human form having a conscious life experience. The universe comes hard-wired with resiliency. It is standard equipment. You arrived into the world with it already inside of you. Inside you there is the power that fashioned all the heavy elements necessary for life on earth after a star imploded cataclysmically. Inside you there is a life force that not only survived, but thrived after five extinctions on our planet. You don't need to conjure up your inner hero. You just need to tap into the heroic energy of a universe that continues to evolve in the face of multiple crises on all fronts.

Core Agreement 7:
Take Responsibility, Receive Freedom

Practice: Shadow work

This requires that we come to terms with what Swiss psychologist Carl Jung called "the shadow." The shadow consists of the emotional trauma and the resulting beliefs about ourselves that we could not integrate because it was too painful. We show great creativity in how we structure our personality in order survive these blows. But in the basement of our unconscious, there lurks all the shadowy energies that we could not allow to surface for fear they might destroy us. And indeed they might have.

If we don't bring the unconscious shadow to the light of consciousness, it will run our lives. To give one personal example of the shadow, I put together a nice-guy personality, quick to understand others, to show compassion and respond to their needs. Some of this reflects my temperament to be sure. But what I've also discovered under all of that is an angry little boy. A big "fuck you" is always ready if I perceive that somebody might reject me. Being a nice guy, I learned not to verbalize this to anybody's face. Rather, I'd just walk away. Fuck you. I don't need you.

So in terms of my shadow work, I needed to do a lot of work to accept that a) I had a lot of unexpressed rage from early trauma and, b) I actually *did* need other people.

Now, when I get triggered, I can catch myself.

Freud said that when the "id" (the unconscious impulse) becomes the "I," we are well on our way to healing and wholeness. The "id" in English is simply the "it," the thing that is running us without our awareness. The "I" is the self that is aware of these impulses, and can therefore take back the reins.

American philosopher Ken Wilber has come up with a model that is helpful. He calls it 3-2-1, where the numbers refer to third person (it), second person (you) and first person (I). Our shadow begins in the first person, as an experience we undergo. But for whatever reason, we cannot live with it and survive. The most common thing we do with this repressed energy is to shift it to the second person – "you." I am not angry, but you are. I am not arrogant, you are. We see it clearly outside of us, on another person. This other person manifests just enough of our shadow that we can feel justified in projecting our own feelings and beliefs on to him/her. If the experience is very traumatic, we dissociate completely and our first person experience becomes an impersonal and sub-human, third-person "it." This manifests as aversions, irrational judgments, phobia, rage, and oversensitivity.

If 1-2-3 is the direction of dissociation, which eventuates in our shadow, the healing process is a matter of reintegration: 3-2-1. We look at our aversion or hypersensitivity (third person "it"), withdraw our projections of our own feelings and judgments from others (second person "you"), and finally own them (first person).

It's important to understand that when we're dealing with the shadow, meditation just makes it worse. We call this spiritual bypassing. Meditation instructions typically include witnessing your mental activity, detaching from that activity, and resting in "no-mind." Which doesn't touch the shadow. It's why there are so many gurus and preachers who get in trouble, acting out sexually or through power plays. They haven't dealt with their shadows and in fact are using spiritual discipline to keep their shadow material unconscious. A spiritual community, whether a church or a sangha, that does not do its shadow work individually and collectively (yes, there is a collective shadow) cannot evolve.

Here are some steps to get at your shadow:

1. Develop your personal lexicon of triggers. In other words, what makes you hyper-reactive? What do you avoid? What causes you to lose it? If you can't bring this to consciousness, ask those who are closest to you. They know, trust me. Make a list of the top three triggers to start with.

   For example:
   - Feeling rejected
   - Feeling unseen and dishonoured
   - Feeling unfairly treated

2. *Identify your feelings* that come up when you get triggered and what you do with those feelings.

   For example:
   When I feel rejected I organize my life so that I reject the other person first. I avoid any situation in which I might be rejected.

I try to be nice to everybody so that I don't ever have to feel rejected. I just *know* the other person is rejecting me.

3. *Face it.* Once you realize what you are feeling and what you typically do with these feelings, you are now able to begin the process of re-integrating the shadow. This will probably mean going deep, with the help of a professional, into the original trauma that you experienced as rejection and that was too much for you to bear.

4. *Own it.* The kenotic practice here is vulnerability. You make a decision that when these feelings come up, you will feel them rather than do what you taught yourself to do when you first felt rejected. Then decide what you will do differently. This might include going to the person who felt was rejecting you, sharing your feelings, and ask whether this was their intention. Then own your vulnerability to feeling rejected, and take responsibility for it.

Having worked this through for one area of your lexicon of triggers, repeat it with the other two. If you are anything like me, you will have more than three triggers and, over time, you can work through them one by one.

By the way, you aren't doing this only for yourself. You are doing this for your loved ones and for the larger spiritual community. When the community is being run by a collective shadow, or the personal shadows of multiple individuals, it is leaking vitality, creativity, and synergy.

Practice: Dream work

Every night when we sleep, we leave our bodies and travel into the realm of creative imagination. In our dream body (astral body), we are not limited by matter, time, or space. We can travel through these dimensions freely. This practice is not so much about interpreting our dreams, as letting our dreams interpret our lives for us. Sometimes it's better to simply allow the images and narrative of the dream live in us over a period of time.

After 30 years of taking my dreams seriously, I believe that dreams function to maintain our health and wholeness, by

- giving us a graphic depiction of the state of our soul
- helping us to come to terms with our deepest fears
- connecting us to higher realms
- showing us what's going on below conscious awareness
- enabling us to be more authentic (dreams don't lie)
- opening up new possibilities
- showing us our unintegrated shadow.

It is in relation to the latter benefit, showing us our shadow, that I believe dreams are particularly important. A nightmare is very often an image of a deep fear we cannot face. For example, I had a dream in which the main protagonist was a Nazi. My therapist asked me to get in touch with my inner Nazi! I thought it was preposterous. I was a nice Christian man. I'm not controlling. I'm certainly not cold-hearted. Certainly I am not capable of murder. Well, actually, as I explored the energy of the Nazi more deeply, I realized that I had so disowned these darker energies within me that my dreams had to go all hyperbolic on me! My dreamer gave me an image that was impossible to ignore.

By the time we are being terrified in our dreams, chances are pretty good that our dreamer (soul) has been trying to get our attention for years, without success. The monster is not there to terrify us, or eat us. It comes to wake us up and get our attention.

Buy a dream journal. Get a nice one that costs a bit of money, to show you are serious. Put it beside your bed with a pen and set a conscious intention to wake up and write your dreams down when they come. We all dream, many times a night. Carl Jung once said that an unexplored dream is like an unopened letter from a long lost friend. It's true. For this practice, pay attention particularly to the unsavoury characters, the monsters, and the images that depict you doing something you wouldn't dream of doing in your waking life.

We will see in the practice of "identifying upper limiting" (below) that it's not always unsavoury characters that define our shadow. I once dreamed that I was the President of the United States. In working with this character, I realized that I was denying my personal power, playing it small and insignificant. This, too, was a shadow dream, and I was being encouraged in my waking life to step up as a leader.

The simplest and most effective method of working with our dreams is to identify with all the characters and symbols. You created them, after all. You *are* these characters. Enter into the character and allow that character to speak *as* you. In the example above, I allowed my inner Nazi to speak and discovered how this energy was dominating a certain aspect of my life.

Practice: Stop complaining

Declare your life and your community a complaint-free zone. Complaint is the refuge of the victim. Stop complaining, once and for all. The reason we complain is that we feel like we are powerless. We want to protest, but assume that the other person has all the power. Instead, make requests. The reason we don't make clear requests is that somewhere along the line we were taught that our wants and needs were not valid. And this became shadow material that surfaces as complaining.

If you don't like something another person is doing, tell them, and then make a request for a change. If they refuse to make the change, which is their right, then you either a) accept the status quo, b) stop expecting that person to act a certain way, c) or walk away. You are free to be in that relationship or not. Complaining is a waste of energy and creativity.

Practice:
Stop jumping to conclusions and start asking questions

When something happens that we don't like and that pisses us off, we make interpretations and assumptions about what just happened. Typically, we do this quickly. The trouble is that we don't often share what those interpretations and conclusions are with the person who has annoyed us. What I've learned over the years is that when somebody does something that makes me feel angry or ashamed, the conclusions and assumptions I come to about what has just happened are almost always wrong. That's because my shadow got triggered.

Instead, share with the other person your interpretation of what just happened. Ask the most vulnerable question you can. (It's the question you don't want to ask.) For example, "When you corrected me in front of the whole class, I feel like you enjoyed humiliating me. Is that true?" Or, "When you came into the room, I felt like you totally ignored me and gave all your attention to Bill. It made me feel small and invisible. Did you do this on purpose?"

This practice only works when we have become competent in dealing with our shadow. Otherwise we won't be sincere in our desire to take responsibility for our feelings. We'll just be using the questions to validate our own assumptions and we won't believe what the other person is telling us anyway.

Practice: No upper-limiting

The shadow can also be comprised of the most talented, gifted, and genius aspects of ourselves. I recall watching an episode of *The White House*. Jed Bartlett is the incredibly bright, Nobel-winning economist, now Democratic president of the U.S.A. He comes to the White House with a liberal agenda, but his staffers begin to notice how often he softens his position and refuses to confront Republican candidates who clearly don't have his chops on the state of the economy or other social issues. His primary speechwriter confronts him, noting that the president's father used to beat him, particularly when Jed was acting too smart. In fact, his staffer points out that Jed was smarter than his father by a long shot, and he was regularly punished whenever his father felt his son's superior mind. So they bring in a New York shrink. The President starts to realize that he upper-limits his genius, for fear of being punished.

In his book *The Big Leap*, psychologist Gay Hendricks gives multiple examples of people who have stopped trying after reaching a certain level of potential because of this dynamic of upper limiting. Upper-limiting is something that most of us can relate to. If we came from large families, where the parents worked hard to make sure that all the children felt equal, there isn't much room for any of children to shine and excel. Children pick up intuitively that it is safer to hold themselves back than to risk surpassing their siblings or their parents. This is also shadow because it is an unconscious impulse that is running our lives by making us less than who we really are. When upper-limiting is reinforced by the false humility that is often cultivated in Christian congregations, leadership is flat-lined, and so much untapped potential is left on the table.

Core Agreement 8:
Surrender to Grace

Then he said to them all, "If any want to become my followers,
let them deny themselves and take up their cross daily and follow me."
– Luke 9:23

I die every day!
– 1 Corinthians 15:31

Surrender

I was recently involved in an ancient shamanic ceremony that originated in the Amazon. It involved consuming a tea that is a purgative. Ahem, it makes you puke. Repeatedly. On the second night of the Big Barf, an intelligence starting teaching me about surrender, while I was emptying the contents of my stomach into a pail. This was the teaching: "You are in control of nothing. You don't even control when you vomit. That is determined for you. You don't control when it starts or when it stops. Your only job right now is to surrender your illusion of control."

This insight transcended intellectual understanding. It wasn't like I was humiliated into getting the teaching. But it continued to register: "Okay, I get it. There are bigger things going on here than my rational mind will ever comprehend, and if I want to participate in the bigger project, I need to give up the illusion of control."

I got that my life was meant to be an offering; I needed to be willing to give over all that is not love to Love itself. I offered everything in me that was getting in the way of love. To paraphrase Amos, this is the only sacrifice that matters ultimately, the only sacrifice that Love wants.

First to the altar was my ego, the self that is not Self – the self that was carefully and ingeniously constructed to compensate for early trauma. This self pretty much ran the show for my entire life. Sobering to say the least. Mind-boggling. Unbelievable, except that I knew it was true. Let me be clear about this. This self isn't bad. It isn't wrong. In fact, I felt more love and compassion and gratitude for this self that helped me to survive than I have ever felt in my life.

When we talk about loving self, it's a real conundrum, because the ego isn't about loving. It's about trying to get in any way possible what you didn't get early in life (unconditional love); or it's about trying to avoid what was intolerable (conditional love). So until we offer up the ego, there is quite literally nobody home to deliver the love we so desperately are looking for. We spend a lifetime looking for this Self and the only way we know that we've found it is if we find ourselves deeply in love with the totality of ourselves, wounds and all. We love our body. We love our minds. We love all the ways we compensated. We love the wounded little guy or girl with such tenderness.

That which is loving like this is our true Self, it's our essential nature.

The ego and the trauma that constitutes the small self is what keeps us believing that we are in control. We must be in control, because if we are not in control we will die. This is how traumatic the absence of unconditional love is. So we come to believe that we control the levers. We might even get into evolutionary spirituality, which is so big on "consciously creating the future." I've taught this myself and I believe it, understood correctly. It's part of the dignity of what it means to be human in the 21st century.

But if it's the ego that is creating the future, we end up, as Bruce Cockburn puts it, with New York, rather than the New Jerusalem. On the other, when we "get it" in our bones that Love itself is building the New Jerusalem 24/7, and that we are being remade every moment of our lives as a kind of on-the-job training through surrender, then our lives begin to feel like they are being lived by a current of Love, who is a master planner. The project is executed in a manner that doesn't violate our sovereignty or freedom, but rather fulfills it. We get that there are higher beings at the controls. Our job is to be reconditioned. We are to trade in the old self for a new model. We are to allow the trauma to be drawn from us, so that we can be remade as new humans who are participating in the emergence of a new earth community.

The moment you get this, a tremendous relief settles you. "Oh, it's not all up to me. I can release into this stream of evolutionary grace that is carrying me toward the completion of love." Breath returns. Maybe laughter. And then our lives truly become an offering, a letting go of all that is not love. It's anything but easy. It's painful. It's unpredictable. It doesn't follow cultural norms or rhythms. It doesn't fit well into the plans that we, or anybody else, have made for ourselves. It doesn't care much for institutional religion. In the immortal words of Lenny Kravitz, it's time to "let love rule."

There was much more to the teaching, and I can tell you that I will never forget it. I reviewed my life and realized the extent to which I thought it was all up to me. I needed to figure it all out in my head. I needed to make all the right decisions. I needed to know everything rationally. I needed to plan my life out carefully. This is what it meant to be responsible. If I just worked harder, then everything would be okay. If I just had enough money…

During the ceremony, it was shown to me that this idea that it was all up to me was illusion, a flight of egoic fancy born of a lack of trust that we are all being lived by a loving intelligence that is sweeping us along in its tide. This intelligence will show us the way, if we but surrender to it.

Jesus knew this when he said to his anxious disciples, "Are not two sparrows sold for only a penny? Yet not one of them will fall to the ground apart from your Father" (Matthew 10:29). And this teaching: "Consider the lilies, how they grow: they neither toil nor spin; yet I tell you, even Solomon in all his glory was not clothed like one of these" (Luke 12:27).

> By virtue of a marvelous mounting force contained in things each
> reality attained and left behind gives us access to the discovery and
> pursuit of an ideal of higher spiritual content. Those who spread their
> sails in the right way to the winds of the earth will always find them-
> selves borne by a current towards the open seas. The more nobly a man

wills and acts, the more avid he becomes for great and sublime aims to pursue. He will no longer be content with family, country and the remunerative aspect of his work. He will want wider organizations to create, new paths to blaze, causes to uphold, truths to discover, an ideal to cherish and defend. So, gradually, the worker no longer belongs to himself. Little by little the great breath of the universe has insinuated itself into him through the fissure of his humble but faithful action, has broadened him, raised him up, borne him on.

—Teilhard de Chardin[6]

I posted this quote on my Facebook page, Home for Evolving Mystics, and Bjorn, one of the members from Sweden, responded incredibly aptly and in a way that captures this agreement and practice:

It's not an individual race, it's a mass movement. Once you find your-self within a larger context, you'll realize you're not moving alone. You have become part of a greater momentum and can relax your personal ambition. You're not going at it alone anymore. Jump into the river and let yourself be swept away. No need to compete as everyone is mov-ing alongside with you, aiding and strengthening the development. Stop worrying about your personal fears and join the whole. All of our individual flaws, our nicks-and-knacks, don't go away, but they are accommodated, cared for and loved, because in the river we all move at the same speed, warts and all. Being in the river is also our *misogi* (a Japanese Shinto practice of ritual purification), our cleansing of our mind's clutter. Our fears are washed away and we can begin to enjoy the ride. Motion is universal and nothing ever stays still for very long. There's a flow to everything; the stars move together, spiraling around the center of the galaxy, the planets around the sun, the Earth around its axis and man around his family and social setting. Find this river in your life and let yourself go.

---

6 Pierre Teilhard de Chardin, The Divine Milieu: An Essay on the Interior Life, trans. William Collins (New York: (Harper and Row, 1965), 50–73.

The more traditional religious language for surrender assumes that G_d's will and our own are essentially different. This is captured in the traditional phrase, "not my will, but thine." But for mystics, there is no sharp dividing line between G_d's essential nature and the rest of creation, including human nature. To make a mistake about creation, said medieval theologian Thomas Aquinas, is to make a mistake about G_d. Nevertheless, in a world in which the illusion of separation prevails, of humans from the rest of nature, of life from death, and G_d from creation, consensus reality shapes individuals, communities, and social-political systems on the assumption of separation. To surrender, then, can feel as though we are relinquishing our natural (bad) nature in order to be ruled by G_d's nature (good).

More helpful images, found in both Teilhard's quote and Bjorn's response above, are those of (spreading) "their sails in the right way to the winds of the earth" and thereby being "borne by a current towards the open seas." Or "jumping into the river and letting yourself be swept away." These images assume an evolutionary current that is carrying the whole universe, and leaving a tapestry of beauty, intelligence, order, and love in its wake. To feel one's life as being swept along by that current has the effect of deepening one's trust that it is not all up to me or you. The universe built itself in an exquisite manner for billions of years, without a human brain. When it produced the human brain, it wasn't for the purpose of taking over the job – at least not from the mind of separation that prevails.

When we overcome this illusion, human intelligence and creativity become one with the current that is carrying us. And when we can relax into this cosmic flow of creativity and love, we are able to create with the mind and heart of Source.

This "relaxing into" is a condition of deep trust that the universe is *for* us. It is not neutral (indifferent) or against us. But this must be a *felt experience* and not simply a rational conclusion. When it becomes a felt experience, then the letting go follows naturally. This basic trust in the goodness and purposefulness of the sacred process that is living us in every moment cannot be manufactured. If trust was broken in our early life, then we will need to do some therapy in order to gain perspective on our distrust and begin the healing process. When trust has been broken, there is a tendency to move our energy to the higher energy centres. Here our mentality can help us to rationalize the idea that we should let go into the Great River, or to spread our sails and be taken by the winds of grace. But under pressure this rarely holds up.

Practice 1

Find a quiet, calm space, preferably at the beginning of the day. Close your eyes and pay attention to your breath for four or five breaths. Imagine yourself on a sailboat on a clear, warm day, with a strong, but not threatening breeze blowing. Now imagine yourself letting up the sails, seeing the sail fill with the breeze, and feel your boat being propelled forward. Notice that it is the wind that is propelling you forward, but you are still steering the boat. Your navigation is crucial, but without the wind you would go nowhere.

Practice 2

Do the breathing exercise, and then begin repeating the phrase "I release into the grace of this day." Set the intention throughout the day to stay alert to experiences that are opportunities to be guided on your path.

Practice 3

Spend the day being alert to small or large synchronicities – occurrences in the outer world that reflect or support a direction or a longing you've had in your inner world.

Practice 4

Do some research to find out whether ecstatic or trance dance is offered in your community. This is unstructured dance, typically to electronic music or percussion. Five Rhythms is one type of class, but there are many more. Dancing in this way allows you to listen to how your body wants to move, and to be led therefore by something other than your rational mind. At first there may be some self-consciousness, but dance is a great way to practice surrender.

Practice 5

If you are married or in an intimate relationship, agree on a day when your partner will be in charge of the agenda for the day. You agree that you will allow this person to determine what you eat, where you eat, where you go during the day, etc. Your role is to entrust the day to your partner. Later you may journal about what it was like not being in control. (Note: for some it is much more difficult to assume control of the day.)

Practice 6

Have your partner stand behind you. Let yourself fall back into his or her arms. Pay attention to the feelings that come up before and after.

Practice 7

Allow yourself to be blindfolded by somebody you trust. Then get them to lead you around the house, or outside. Pay attention to the feelings that arise. What is it like to surrender control to another?

── TEN ──

EVOLUTIONARY MIDRASH:

The Garden of Eden and the Prodigal Son as Creation Stories

Every blade of grass has an angel whispering in its ear, "Grow, grow, grow."
— The Talmud

From envelopment to development

What follows is an interpretation of two foundational biblical stories using an evolutionary lens through as an interpretive tool. First, I will look at the story of Adam and Eve in Genesis. Then I will move to the story of the prodigal son in the New Testament.

Background

One way to understand evolution is as a dynamic process that proceeds through envelopment and development. Viewed in this way, we can treat each of these stories as a kind of creation story. We need to keep in mind that the scientific story of creation, the evolutionary process, is on-going. It is a cosmo-genesis, a rebirthing moment by moment, and not a once upon a time event that happened way back then. We need to understand this dynamic of envel-opment and de-velopment as an evolutionary dynamic that drives the process by which novel forms, consciousness, and cultures emerge.

Harvard psychologist Robert Kegan is one of the world's foremost authorities on how the self evolves. In his book *The Evolving Self,* he describes the process of self-evolution or development. While we often talk about the "self" as though it is a discrete and static entity located somewhere within our brains, in actuality we don't have this kind of self. Rather, we are the personalized expression of a "selfing" *process.* We are a process of development that evolves through distinct and measurable stages of human development.

To put it another way, it is more accurate to say that we are humans *becoming* rather than human beings. And you will by now know my bias that we are humans on the way to realizing the True Human. The history of humanity is the history of our species acquiring new intelligences in response to shifting life conditions. These intelligences emerge as ever-evolving worldviews – core beliefs, values, assumptions about the nature of reality, narratives and cosmologies, along with art, artifact, technologies, and modes of governance. The self we identify with is mediated through these filters. We are always in the process of becoming. It is true that during a particular phase of this ceaseless becoming, we are at rest sufficiently to give the sense of endurance – which gives us a feeling of being a self that endures through time.

That we are in constant motion does not mean that there is no coherent organizing intelligence. This we could perhaps call the Self, which enables those of us who enjoy *relative* psychological health to arrive at adulthood able to function more or less effectively. Another way to say this is that we are the personalization of a self-organizing intelligence, and this self-organizing intelligence is one of the mysteries of the universe. Our participation in this field of self-organizing intelligence gives rise to a sense of self.

So how does this selfing process evolve? Kegan describes how we find ourselves throughout life in what he calls "holding environments." These holding environments are mother, mother/father, family, peers, schools, workplaces, and society at large. The primary holding environment is, of course, nature herself, Mother Earth. The word I am using for these holding environments is "envelope." I am grateful to Belgian embryologist Jaap van der Wal for this take on envelopment and development.

These holding environments are the envelopes that enclose us. Kegan says that there are three primary functions of a healthy holding environment:

- **Holding** (signalling that this is a safe environment to identify with)
- **Letting go** (signalling that one's need to differentiate is welcome)
- **Challenging** (signalling that that it's time to move on, when we are linger too long in the envelope or holding environment).

These holding environments or envelopes can either serve or impede the evolutionary process. Cultures of love foster development of self, whereas cultures of shame impede. Shame, we will see, figures prominently in the story of the first couple in Genesis, whereas love is the holding environment in the parable of the prodigal son.

The "I" of one stage becomes the "me" of the "I" of the next stage of development

To review, the holding environment is meant to hold, to let go, and to challenge. When the holding environment is "good enough" (Winnicott) our Self is able to evolve to the next stage of development. The proximate "me" (the self I think of as "me") that I had previously identified with now becomes distal. It's now "out there." I can look at it and reflect on it. I am no longer identified with that self. That self has a context. What was once interior and invisible (the subject) now becomes exterior to me and visible (the object). The "I" of one stage becomes the "me" of the "I" of the next stage of development. What was subjective now becomes objective. I have de-veloped, emerged out of that which en-veloped me. A new emergence of the selfing process has hatched.

I regard each occasion of development as a creation story, a kind of death and rebirth of self. The self that emerges transcends, yet includes, the previous sense of self. This is the selfing process, the evolution of self, which should naturally continue throughout a lifetime, right up until death (and beyond).

This kind of envelopment, which gives way to development, happens as well on a collective level. Let's call this collective level "culture." Cultures are collectives comprised of people who share a similar worldview. A worldview is a perspective on life. It is made up of shared beliefs, values, and ways of interpreting or making sense of reality. Here are some worldviews that have emerged throughout history. Again, each worldview is a kind of envelope that, when healthy, provides a holding function, a challenging function, and finally a letting go into a new or emergent worldview. I present these worldviews in more depth in my book, *The Emerging Church: A Model for Change and a Map for Renewal*. These emergent cultures are

- Archaic
- Premodern (Magic, Tribal, and Traditional)
- Modern
- Postmodern
- Integral (Post-postmodern)

As we move into the story of creation in Genesis, we need to keep in mind the Bible was written from within the worldview of a pre-modern consciousness. A pre-modern culture is not an unsophisticated culture. These cultures possess timeless wisdom and forms of intelligence that need to be carried forward into the 21st century and beyond. On the other hand, these worldviews are limited in some ways. The Bible reflects the core concerns of a premodern (traditional) worldview – a preoccupation, for example, with obedience to authority as the key to moral order, located in the One, True, and Unchanging G_d. The good will be rewarded and the evil will be punished by this God.

The Garden of Eden

Over the past 30 years I have tried to redeem the story of the first couple as a reflection of timeless wisdom. I have used allegory, metaphor, and mystical interpretations. But when I gave up trying to redeem it and let it be an expression of the worldview through which it was written, a new and more organic interpretation emerged.

When I read the story of the first couple through the lens of this evolutionary dynamic of envelopment and the impulse for de-velopment – in other words, the natural human impulse to emerge from the envelope of the dominant culture, worldview, and personal identity – I can't help but see a story that reflected the holding environment that was appropriate for the value system of a traditional worldview. But to ascribe to it the same authority in a post-21st century context impedes the sacred impulse to evolve.

It is a story written by representatives – likely priests and scribes – of a traditional worldview, a religious system whose primary, even exclusive, concern is with the preservation of a particular order. The legitimate concern of this traditional worldview is to establish moral order and to live in accordance with God's will – interpreted as an unchanging order requiring above all obedience to external authority.

In this worldview, a single G_d is in charge of life, and while it is beyond our capacity to understand "His" ways, the way to know Him is through obedience to divine law and the moral codes that He has established. Essentially, the traditional worldview is concerned with taming or domesticating the twin evolutionary impulses for love and adventure. Think about the main character in *Fiddler on the Roof*, Tevya. Remember the song "Tradition"? You don't ask questions; you just stay within the prescribed limits of the society. Again, there is nothing inherently wrong with a traditional worldview. It expresses a particular kind of intelligence. But this intelligence needs to be incorporated within the context of later worldviews.

The traditional cultural worldview establishes clear boundaries around what is right and wrong, true and false. It is deeply suspicious of what is natural, wild, and undomesticated. This includes a suspicion of our deepest longings for more – more love, more adventure, or more beauty. The primary spiritual orientation is one of submission to a pre-established divine order. By strict adherence to the codes of the religion, you will prosper. Fear of punishment is a primary motivator for obedience.

Again, the myth of Adam and Eve is written from the unconscious assumptions associated with a traditional religious worldview. This doesn't make it "wrong" necessarily. But history shows that it *can be* disastrous when it is used by the dominant culture as a tool of control, as it has been historically.

The traditional Christian interpretation of the Garden of Eden story sees it as a fall/redemption story. The fall from grace – an unself-conscious union with G_d – is caused by an act of disobedience. Eve succumbs to the serpent's temptation by taking the forbidden fruit, thus overreaching human limitations. She makes an incursion into the divine domain, blurring the boundaries between human and divine. The stated concern of G_d or the gods regarding this action is what?

It is the fear that the couple will gain conscious awareness (their eyes will be opened) and that they will gain the capacity to know the difference between good and evil – but not because some external authority told them so. They will know it from within. And this, in the mind of the writers or compilers for the story, is dangerous.

The writers are also concerned that they will then eat of the tree of eternal life – again, overstepping the "natural" limitations of humans, who thereby are making an incursion into the divine realm. As a consequence of eating the forbidden fruit, they are banished from the garden into a life of toil, painful childbirth, and are required to deal with the sufferings associated with mortality.

This interpretation has supported, among other unfortunate consequences, the oppression of women as temptresses of innocent men. In turn, traditional Christian interpretations "solve" the problem of the fall and original sin with the atoning death of Jesus. Through his blood we are "redeemed" back into a state of grace and are granted eternal life. (Ironically, eternal life is precisely what the gods are *not* willing to grant in the myth of Eden. They banish the first couple before they are tempted to eat of the fruit of the tree of life, which would confer immortality.)

Through the interpretive lens of a traditional worldview, Christianity consists of behaving properly, obeying G_d, knowing your place, believing the right things (that Jesus died for your sins), and receiving the gift of eternal life. Jesus removes the curse of this original sin and we are liberated.

As I've said, this traditional understanding continues to serve many (actually most) Christians. It's strength is in the way it speaks to an intuitive sense that the human condition is far from ideal, in need of redemption, and that we are indeed trying to "get back to the garden," as Joni Mitchell put it. As well, it speaks to the importance of limits and of the ego's need to be able to take direction.

But based on the aforementioned premise that one of the primary directives of a traditional worldview is to reign in natural impulses, it strikes me that in the myth G_d (or the gods – *Elohim*) is actually a projection of our deep fear of a natural, primordial, and sacred desire to reach out for more, to go beyond our current condition – in other words to evolve. This is an impulse that is unique to human creatures. Other creatures have reached a state of perfection. Without the capacity for conscious self-awareness, they will be what they will be, for all eternity. Their form and function is therefore, perfected. They feel no desire for transcendence. In the story, G_d is a projection of what Freud would call the superego, the part of us that has internalized culture's anxiety about our wild, animal nature, and Nature in general.

This is not so much a critique of the traditional worldview as it is an observation that this worldview emerged, in part, to solve the very real life condition of the previous worldview of the *warrior*, and the anarchy and violence this loosed upon the world. Ironically, the traditional worldview itself became a domination narrative of the ruling class in the Western world. Starting in the fourth century, the Christian narrative was used as a monological and ideological tool of control for empire.

The Garden of Eden as holding environment

The Garden of Eden, or Paradise, seems like the quintessential holding environment. Certainly it has come down to us in the tradition as such. Adam is well taken care of, every need provided for, and when it is perceived that he needs a helpmate, Eve is created out of his rib. The first couple lives in a state of equanimity and bliss, no suffering. As long as they follow the rules – actually rule, singular, because there really is only one: do not eat of the tree of the knowledge of good and evil. If they do this, everything will be fine.

This doesn't seem onerous until you realize that it's the fundamental rule of all traditional religious systems. Do not trust your own experience as the basis for wisdom and guidance in life. Look to the priests. Look to the Pope. Look to the commandments. Look outside yourself for wisdom. The story says that this is the explicit concern of the gods. If the first couple's eyes are opened, they will become like the gods – who presumably enjoy the freedom to live by their own rules.

Everything is fine until Eve sees the fruit that is forbidden food. It is alluring. It looks good to eat. She wants it. Here we are dealing with a fundamental mystery of human existence, which this myth also attempts to address from a traditional worldview. Why do we want more? Why can't we settle for good enough? Why do we want better? And I'm not necessarily talking about the desire for more that issues from a felt sense of insufficiency. This can be trouble, as we know. "How much money do we need?" an interviewer once asked billionaire Richard Branson. "Just a little more," was his response. Here we need to recall the difference between egoic desire, or craving, and holy longing. The longing for more freedom, love, joy, and agency fall into the latter category.

But Eve didn't reach out, in my opinion, from a sense that there was anything missing. All her basic needs were met. And that is precisely the point. The story of evolution is precisely the story (as Abraham Maslow showed in his research) that once our basic survival or physiological needs for sustenance and sex are met, our soul is liberated to ask the question, "Okay, great, but what's next?" There is a consciousness dividend. Our attention is liberated to focus higher up the pyramid of motivational impulses. *Eve doesn't reach out because of lack, but because she is full* – she is fulfilled at a basic, survival, level of existence.

Eve, in my interpretation, is doing something essentially different from modern Western culture. We in the modern world are tempted to what Walter Wink called the "regressive alternative." We don't reach for the greater, the deeper, the more beautiful, the transcendent. Rather, we reach for more of the same. We already have our basic needs taken care of, but we keep reaching out for more of the same thing: more sex (the proliferation of pornography); more food (the epidemic of obesity); more wealth (the psychopathy of corporations); more luxury (affluenza), and the pathology of killing ourselves by overwork, not to mention destroying our Mother who feeds us). Our yearning for more of what we already have is a deeply pathological yearning.

But our souls are not the least bit interested in this kind of more. The soul is no longer allured by mere procreation, but by co-creation; no longer by material security, but by the promise of deep spiritual adventure; the soul is no longer interested in the superficial community life that we call church, but by a deeper intimacy.

Eve's reaching out comes from this kind of holy longing, a yearning to exit the (now) stultifying envelope of Paradise. She desires to de-velope, to get outside the protective envelope and discover an unprotected life. She's looking for, "What's next?" But in a traditional worldview, *there is no next*, at least not at the initiative of humans. There is only obedience through the divine order, and thereby G_d will determine what is next.

But notice in this myth the nature and characteristics of G_d or the gods. In this creation myth, G_d is anxious, controlling, and punishing of the natural impulse of Eve to eat what looks like good fruit. She wants to possess an innate wisdom. The fact that it is the first woman who reaches out suggests as well that the dominant culture of patriarchy felt the need to control all that we associate with the feminine – intuition, orienting to the world through the sensual, receptive, nurturing, a greater capacity to integrate desire in a healthy way into the human condition. In fact, this could describe Christianity's attitude historically toward the feminine, toward nature, toward the body and our senses.

The subservience of women is presented as a consequence of Eve's disobedience. By incorporating this story of women being derivative of men (she is formed from the rib of Adam) into a creation narrative, it ensured that the wild, feminine would not threaten the "divine order," which in truth is not a divine order, but merely patriarchy.

G_d, in other words, is a projection of the priestly writer's consciousness. And these writers are invested, not in de-velopment, but in making an airtight envelope. What they *don't* want is the birth of a new order. They want subservience to the existing order. Ultimately, this need to freeze the process of evolution is futile. It's like a mother trying to stop the birth once her water has broken. The only way to control it is through the threat of terrible violence, which is, in many ways the story of human history.

For most spiritual communities, including the church, the envelope is too strong. They need to get out of their envelope, to reach for the forbidden fruit. In the end, no Pope, no regime, no dictator can enact sufficient violence to prevent the birth that wants to happen from happening. The tide of evolution will eventually sweep away all dams along with their engineers and architects.

I am interpreting "G_d" in the myth as a projection of the traditional worldview's fear of the wild, the feminine, the natural, and of a healthy desire in the human for "more," for whatever is next. To take this one step further, the traditional worldview is threatened by conscious awareness itself – G_d does not want the eyes of the couple to be open, a clear metaphor of conscious self-awareness, which itself is expansive. Consciousness wants to expand and see the world through multiple perspectives.

The "serpent," according to the traditional worldview of the writers, embodies the evil temptation to expand one's consciousness, to step outside the prevailing set of assumptions associated with the dominant worldview and discover that you can actually survive outside the "garden" of the dominant culture. The serpent is pro de-velopment.

The serpent is called crafty. The word derives from an old German word *kriefteg*, which originally meant ingenious, original, and creative. Not until the 16th century did *kriefteg* gain the additional meaning of deceptive. In this etymological addition, we can perhaps get a whiff of traditional Christianity's suspicion of creativity – in particular of the urge to create oneself, to know directly, to experience life with immediacy, that is, unmediated by a priesthood and its tradition. Mystics, in this sense, would be considered crafty. Women who refused to be domesticated would also be considered "crafty."

The snake whispers to Eve, "Actually, Eve, you won't die. I know the gods said you will, but it's a lie. They are just worried that you will become like them and share their creative power and authority." And, of course, the snake is actually telling the truth. But the writers of the creation myth deal with this by interpreting death itself not as a natural condition, but as a punishment for daring to become conscious.

The snake, then, in my interpretation, is actually G_d, the subver-

sive, creative impulse to differentiate from the dominant culture, meta-phorically the garden of our unconscious identification with the pre-vailing worldview.

In other words, the explicit purpose of the myth is to freeze the evolution of consciousness at a traditional worldview. It's like a mother who doesn't want her children to grow up. The holding environment in this case is a religious system unconsciously, or perhaps consciously, invested in keeping the children from growing up.

The snake, however, is the *true* G_d whispering in our ear to not be afraid. "Every blade of grass," the Talmud claims, "has an angel whispering in its year, "Grow, grow, grow..." The snake is an ambassador of the culture that is awaiting the first couple outside the garden gates of unconscious obedience to external authority. I'm delighted that the snake snuck into the story under the radar as a subversive presence. When the envelope is too tight, the Real slips into the myth subversively.

But the implications of the myth as it is told are chilling and far-reaching. History itself is understood – perhaps not consciously – as a punishment. It is not an adventure into an unknown future, not an opportunity to realize deeper expressions of love, not an opportunity to co-create with Spirit the "world that our hearts know is possible," to use Charles Eisenstein's phrase, but a punishment. According to the myth as traditionally interpreted, there is something essentially wrong with us that needs to be redeemed.

Evolution is a series of irreversible transformations, in the words of Thomas Berry, which he actually got from Catholic priest and paleontologist Teilhard de Chardin. This doesn't mean that there is no incorporation of all that has come before. This is actually how evolution proceeds – by transcending, but including, all that is in the service of life. But there is no Golden Age that lies in the past. There are ways of being, skills that can and should be carried forward and enacted, intelligences that we would do well to integrate, yes. (I'll say more about this when we get to the parable of the prodigal son, but I believe that we're in the midst of a reclamation of indigenous skills and practices that modernity forgot, much to our detriment.)

There is a detail in the creation myth that I think is brilliant: specifically, that the gates of the garden are guarded by cherubim with flaming swords. There is no going back into the envelope. Evolution, as I just said, is a series of *irreversible* transformations. We can experience this exit as either one of joyful and ecstatic opportunity, or as shameful banishment. A healthy holding environment results in the former. An unhealthy holding environment results in the latter. Actually, the interpretation of this historical process as punishment, rather than as blessing, can only come from a prior experience of shame and separation – from the largely unredeemed trauma of felt separation from the cosmos, Earth, G_d, the creatures, and our essential nature. This is why the mystic orientation requires us to deal with shame in order to reclaim the primordial unity with All That Is.

Literature is filled with stories about courageous folk who dared to follow their soul's curiosity and urge for more beauty, truth, and goodness by reaching out for the fruit that was forbidden by their culture. I think of Miriam Toews' novel *A Complicated Kindness*. It tells the story of an orthodox Mennonite family who lived on the edges of that culture, and lived daily with the shame that was enacted upon them by the community after they were shunned. Copernicus, Galileo, Giordano Bruno, women who were considered to be witches, feminists such as Betty Friedan, Rosa Parks, Martin Luther King Jr., Bishop Romero, Nelson Mandela – all of these individuals embodied the cultural longing to reach out for more, and were summarily shamed and/or put to death.

The story of the first couple's banishment is a story of shame. The banishment is effectively a shunning, a punishment for following a natural, evolutionary impulse. The creation myth represents a response to the very trauma of dissociation – from Earth, from the body, and from G_d. The gods or G_d are motivated by fear, not love. They are jealous that the couple's eyes will be opened and they will have to share knowledge and wisdom and eternal life with the humans. They are keeping an unnatural hierarchy in place, which itself reflects a former trauma in the lives and history of the writers of this story.

The presence of shame freezes the evolutionary trajectory in the human domain. It is the most effective strategy to seal the envelope and prevent de-velopment. To return to Kegan's theory, holding environments serve three functions: to hold, to let go, and to challenge. This story of the first couple might appear as an instance of the third function, challenge. But it's not, in that the couple, by their sharing of the forbidden fruit, was good and ready to de-velope.

Banishment is not "loving challenge." It's not a parent saying to a young adult, "You know, it's really time that you moved out, stood on your own two feet, or if you are going to live here, you need to contribute to the household." Banishment is a shaming strategy. The only means of survival, in cultures of honour and shame, is to follow the rules and norms. When you are cast out, you are economically and emotionally vulnerable. Cast out from that culture, you are under-resourced to survive outside the gates. Much of the gospel story is focused on Jesus' befriending of these *anawim* (the little ones), who were the shamed of society. The fear of banishment ensures that only one of the functions of the holding environment prevails, and that is to *hold* and not allow to evolution or de-velopment.

A modern-day Garden of Eden myth

In the film *The Matrix*, the protagonist, Neo, is part of a world in which his every need is provided. He is comfortable, has enough food to eat, a decent job. There is no suffering. It is, in this sense, a kind of Garden of Eden. But something isn't right. He intuits that something is amiss. What he doesn't know, but vaguely feels, is that his job as a computer programmer is actually in service to a program that is generated by the Matrix. The Matrix is kept in place by machines. The system is the equivalent of a fundamentalist religious culture. Or you could also say, an economic system that is ideologically fundamentalist in its own way. It aims to keep the people unconscious. The Romans had a term for their own system, which was designed to do exactly the same thing. They called "bread and circuses." Acquire power and popularity, while keeping the masses in a spell and under control, by offering food and entertainment.

They'll never revolt. They'll stay passive. The Wachowski brothers, who wrote and directed the film, were very aware that they were creating a failed holding environment when they imagined *The Matrix*.

But there arises an underground resistance movement. Neo is visited by Morpheus, one of the leaders of the resistance. The name Morpheus means to change, to morph, to evolve. This character is all about supporting the movement in the direction of the service of greater life and freedom. After explaining carefully that Neo exists in a sealed envelope generated by a computer program, Morpheus challenges Neo. He presents him with two pills. One of them will confer conscious awareness. He eyes will be opened. But there is a cost. He will exit his comfortable life forever. There will be no going back. He will enter real history, which will be a life of suffering and resistance, but it will be real. This is not a threat. It's not a punishment. There will be no shaming, just an invitation to join the real world. It's a choice. The other pill will take him back into the Matrix, where he can live comfortably, but in a spell of ignorance, for the rest of his life.

The Matrix is a modern-day Garden of Eden story. It is a creation story for our age. Morpheus offers a healthy holding environment that fulfills all the conditions of such. It holds Neo while he comes to conscious awareness, preparing him for his mission. The holding environment of the resistance movement will give him the training necessary to de-velope. It will release him when the time is right, and it will challenge him repeatedly to step into his larger identity – to assume the role of redeeming the Matrix, and liberating the people.

* * * * *

When I gave up trying to redeem the Garden of Eden creation story, it actually seemed to be the opposite – an anti-creation story. It is the story of a culture that warned against the perils of de-velopment. "God," as identified by the writers, is actually a projection of the fear of the writers and editors, who are enveloped by a traditional religious consciousness.

The snake, on the other hand, is actually, really G_d. The snake after all, tells the truth. The couple doesn't die. The gods are simply afraid that the human beings have the potential to become gods. The snake challenges the first couple to grow in awareness, to evolve.

This story continues to be played out when fundamentalist religions warn against the perils of modernity, and, in the case of militant Islam, are willing to enact terrible violence to generate fear. It is played out when modernist capitalist cultures are "invested" in keeping our eyes shut to the violence that this worldview enacts upon Earth. It is played out when modern materialist science gangs up on the likes of biologist Rupert Sheldrake, after his TEDx talk. When any particular worldview or holding environment refuses development and uses fear and shame to preserve its own envelope, it does not represent the God of evolution and development.

Eve (the feminine aspect of both men and women) becomes the heroine, reaching out to take the forbidden fruit (the erotic catalyst) that allows the power of abundant life (the fruit of the tree of life) to animate us. These powers are the sacred evolutionary impulse itself moving through us to transcend existing (unconscious) conditions, making it possible for us to align ourselves with the sacred trajectory of a Spirit-infused universe that is yearning for an increase in beauty, truth, and goodness. This erotic impulse is in search of a more liberated culture to express its boundless creativity and love.

Eve represents the unconscious power of the feminine divine within cultures that have become too restrictive. She represents this power rising up and reaching out *in subversion* of the voices that would prevent our natural evolution in and toward the alluring Heart of G_d, and ultimately *to realize,* consciously, that all of this wondrous diversity is unfolding and converging within the One, Unified and Unifying Source. The goal of the spiritual life, then, is not about redemption from a fall, but rather about consenting to be liberated from cultures that restrict the soul's restless yearning to fashion a world that our hearts know is possible. We'll end up outside the gates of the Garden of Bliss and in the realm of an unfolding history that involves suffering, yes, but we'll find ourselves (actually) animated by a promise that is only for those who dare to reach out and take the forbidden fruit.

The Garden of Eden story is useful in the way that it gives us a snapshot of a particular kind of culture. Its symbols and metaphors reveal the mechanics of a culture dedicated to eliciting allegiance and keeping our eyes shut – a culture that has fallen in love with its envelope. In truth, what needs redemption is not a presumed fall from grace, and its various solutions, including the Jesus fix. What needs redemption are the cultures of fear and shame that wish to freeze the evolutionary impulse that otherwise would allure us towards deeper expressions of beauty, truth, and goodness.

The Prodigal Son

The holding environment depicted in the parable is the father's heart. As we've seen, a good enough holding environment serves three functions: to hold, to let go, and, when necessary, to *challenge* – to push out of the nest. My basic premise is that this parable is actually a creation story, whereas the creation story related to the first couple, Adam and Eve, is an anti-creation story. The story of the prodigal son describes a good enough habitat for a natural process of evolutionary emergence to occur. The son exits the envelope of a loving culture in order to discover for himself what is next outside that envelope – in other words, he exits in order to develop.

The story begins with the son asking for his inheritance. The father doesn't resist for a moment. The father does not shame, issues no warnings, and utters no threats of punishment in the face of the son's urge to differentiate. The father confers the gift of freedom upon the son. He releases him. There are no speeches about being foolish. The releasing includes resourcing the son for his adventure – meeting the son's request to receive his inheritance now.

The son's request to receive his portion of the inheritance and to leave the holding environment of the dominant culture is the equivalent of reaching for the forbidden fruit in Eden. According to Jewish law, this inheritance rightfully belonged to the eldest son, who at the father's death, decided how to divide it. The youngest son makes an outrageous request, reaching for what is not rightfully his. In granting the request, the father breaks Jewish law.

The son is responding to a felt need for more than this holding environment can offer. Poet David Whyte writes that anything or anybody that does not bring you joy is too small for you. What impulse, we might ask, has ignited a yearning in him? Again, it is the same impulse that caused Eve to want more – a holy longing for more. As with the story of the Garden of Eden, this is not because of a felt sense of insufficiency; the holding environment is meeting his basic needs. We can see from the father's behaviour that it is a loving and generous environment. The son's yearning, then, is not the yearning of an insatiable ego. Rather, with his needs for security and stability having been provided for, a soul yearning is liberated. He reaches out to take what the envelope of the prevailing culture considered forbidden.

This yearning is what choreographer Martha Graham called the *blessed unrest*, or the divine dissatisfaction. To be in this yearning is itself to participate in the yearning of G_d for realization. Yearning in this sense is the predisposition of the mystic.

As the son leaves one holding environment, he is going to be initiated into another one. But let's not be naïve about these initiations into a new order of being, stage of development, or new reality. Becoming a new creation is gritty business. The ancients used ordeal to mark the shift into a new development stage, say from adolescence into adulthood, or womanhood into motherhood. The ceremonies were demanding. Jesus himself ceremonialized his shift into public ministry by leaving society and going into the wilderness. In fact, one version of the story says that he was *driven* there by Spirit.

And once in the wilderness, Jesus was required to deal with Satan. In today's psychological language, we might call Satan our *shadow* – all those disowned aspects of ourselves that we push down into the darkness of our subconscious. For Jesus, the shadow was love of power, money, and status. He was sorely tested. Satan always tempts toward the "regressive alternative," the alternative that freezes evolution.

So, yes, the prodigal son will be tested. He will go through an ordeal to prepare him to take his next evolutionary step into the True Human. Along the way, the prodigal son takes some missteps. There are no guarantees in this evolution into full human maturity. He has soon squandered the inheritance, as we humans are in the process of doing on Earth. His indignity is absolute. A Jew serving a Gentile, a Jew not only feeding pigs, but wishing he could eat the pig food so great was his hunger. He was in a state of impurity according to Jewish law.

His particular spiritual lesson, in my reading, was humility. Perhaps he needed to experience firsthand what poverty was like. Perhaps there was a layer of entitlement in his personality that needed to be purged. The universe is a great teacher. Our souls came to learn something specific, and we shape our lives to give us the experiences we need in order to evolve as souls. The son finds himself in a state of despair, of genuine grief for what he has done. He enters into a process of radical self-inquiry, something that is also required at this juncture of our species. It is his wilderness time. In our own personal lives, there must be time for wilderness – times when we must make a thorough inventory of how our choices may have led to unnecessary suffering and grief.

The line of the text upon which the story pivots, in my opinion, captures the results of this self-inquiry. "He came to his senses." I don't take this to mean that the son regrets acting upon his impulse to reach out and risk life outside the holding environment of his family, his culture, and his religion. But I *do* think he is about to learn what his soul came to learn.

If we look beyond the personal implications of this story, at the level of cultural evolution, the story is a metaphor for the journey that humans took away from a premodern worldview into modernism. This de-velopment from the envelope or holding environment of the premodern or traditional world-view was necessary, but it has not been easy. It started approximately 300 years ago and is associated with the Enlightenment and with the Industrial Revolution. Our species began to see Earth as primarily a resource or a commodity to be exploited by humans, and, for the first time in history, gained the technological expertise to once and for all dominate the natural world. It has left us with a legacy of pollution, overpopulation, and consumerism.

We are just now beginning to exit the modern worldview, having discovered that it is no longer sustainable. Rather than honouring the inheritance of

13.8 billion years of cosmic evolution, and 4.5 billion years of planetary abundance, we have acted like the prodigal species, and squandered the inheritance. Now we are making a deep self-inquiry as a species. We are, I hope, coming to our senses. The modernist focus on achievement, technological progress, and science have been positive in many ways. We were able to transcend many superstitions, make many medical and technological breakthroughs that have served humanity well. But because we did not have the means or the inclination to honour the inheritance, we find ourselves in a condition of deep indignity – living on a planet that is daily being degraded by our presence.

Part of the practice of coming to our senses, then, as a species and as individuals, is to deeply honour, rather than squander, our inheritance, even as we step forward into the future that is calling us. It is to learn and embody the "Great Story" of 13.8 billion years of evolution as our own sacred inheritance. In doing so, we include in our honouring our cosmological kin, the galaxies and the stars, and our biological kin, right down to the bacteria in our gut.

From the perspective of the Great Story of our universe, the inheritance represents 13.8 billion years of evolution in the cosmological, biological, social-cultural domains. In my book *Darwin, Divinity, and the Dance of the Cosmos*, I interpret the story as the Parable of the Prodigal Species. In the past 400 to 500 years, the age of modernity, our species took the inheritance of Earth, cosmos, and all our ancestors – human and other-than-human – and left the enveloping culture of traditional Christianity and even, I would say, the enveloping culture of our bodies, and Earth. We acted as *takers*, not as grateful *receivers* of the inheritance, and did what the prodigal son did – squandered it in irresolute living.

We treated Earth, her biosystems, and our own bodies *instrumentally*. We regarded these are mechanistic means to economic ends. Everything and everybody became a commodity, a resource to serve our ends. And, of course, we ended up as the prodigal species – in a state of indignity and enacting indignities upon our one Earth community. We left the enveloping culture of traditional Christianity, we differentiated ourselves from the planet and other species. But the differentiation descended into dissociation. And now we're locked into an unhealthy expression of modernist culture, an envelope that is now smothering us.

In the parable, the son "comes to his senses." I take the phrase literally in terms of our development and evolution. We are being challenged to literally re-incorporate as a species, to re-embody our experience. What was lost ever since the Cartesian split between mind/soul and body, when the mind was subsequently privileged over the body and ultimately over Earth herself, was the deep intelligence of the body and the deep intelligence of the living organism that is Earth. The way home as a species involves becoming willing to feel again – to come to our senses of touch, sight, hearing, smell, and taste.

"Coming to our senses," as a species, means being led directly into the trauma that caused us to be so dissociated in the first place. It means feeling into it, knowing that the way *out* is *through*. Our fully alive, fully open, fully loving hearts will not be awakened until we have come to our senses. And any talk of development, of the evolution of our species, that does not come from the heart will simply increase the trauma.

The prodigal son finds his heart. He discovers the immensity of the inheritance that he has up to this point squandered. He discovers how alienated he is. He rehearses his repentance speech and prepares to return home.

The prodigal son's homecoming is not merely a return to the old envelopment or holding environment. Evolution, as I said, is a series of irreversible transformations and the myth of the first couple got this much right – there is no returning to the Garden which you left or from which you were banished. If it is merely a return, it is a de-volution. It goes against the erotic impulse of the creative process itself.

Remember, because this is a true creation story the prodigal is not returning from a banishment, but rather from a paternal blessing. His remorse is different from shame. Shame freezes the evolutionary process. It causes a child to return to mother, father, family with the prepared speech, "I'll be good. I'll be better. I know I was bad, but I'll try harder." With shame, the only strategy is to behave better within a holding environment that does not want you to be your radiant and, dare I say, wild, erotic self. Rather, it just wants you to fit in. The prodigal son's repentance is not aimed at appeasing a rejecting father. It is a hard-won repentance that is born of an awakening. He is ready now to evolve.

As mentioned in an earlier chapter, I have detected in evolutionary thinkers, and even in my own thinking, a little too much heroism. There is too much of a sense that we are penetrating our world with our genius, that the past is past, and we need to focus exclusively on the glorious future of our engineering.

But if we imagine that evolution is not about our engineering of the future, but about allowing the past intelligences of human and other-than-human creation to inform that future, we engage in a gesture of honouring our inheritance, while participating in the emergence of a new future.

So why did the father run to greet the son? He probably ran in order to get to his son *before* he entered the village. The father runs in an effort to get to his son before the community gets to him, so that his son does not experience the shame and humiliation of their taunting and rejection. The village would have followed the running father, would have witnessed what took place at the edge of the village between father and son. After this emotional reuniting of the prodigal son with his father, it was clear that there would be no *kezazah* ceremony[1]; there would be no rejecting this son, no shaming ritual.

The father's love becomes a new holding environment for the son to continue his development, his evolution. He literally envelopes the son in his arms and then plans for a great celebration. It's important to appreciate that the son returns with a new identity and a new orientation. He no longer regards himself as a privileged and entitled son, but rather he knows himself to be a servant. He has undergone what we have described as *metanoia*. He has attained a higher mind than the one with which he left home. Through his death and re-birth, he has attained the mind of Christ. This acquiring of humility, then, is his fundamental evolutionary advance, bringing him closer to the goal of love, exemplified by his father.

---

1 In first-century Palestine, if a son squandered a family inheritance, the village would come to him with a pot and break it, signifying his alienation from the village.

The question, likewise, for our species is whether we are willing to let go of our assumed privileged status on Earth and become servants of the One Earth Community – givers, and not merely takers. We need to develop from our state of adolescence as a species; we need to grow up to the next stage of our development. This is what I think Jesus' ministry was about – helping us to grow up and to step up on behalf of our planet before it's too late.

The attitude of the elder son is a nice touch. He symbolizes the resentment and bitterness of those who choose to remain safely ensconced in the same holding environment and who never reach out for more. Like Martha, he is the obedient one, who followed the rules, the faithful son who didn't go for the fruit. He plays the role of the orthodox G_d in the Garden of Eden. He is punishing and shaming. Notice, however, that the father doesn't shame the elder son either.

We all have a right to be exactly where we are, evolutionarily speaking. The elder son has chosen his path, as is his right. The father simply asks him to assume responsibility for choosing to stay home, and thereby be able to join in the celebration of the one who has returned. Like Martha, the elder son resents his younger brother's greater freedom.

We have looked at two creation stories, one in Genesis and another in the story of the prodigal son. We now know from science that a true creation story is an evolutionary story. There must be movement, de-velopment, and an affirmation that as humans we are meant to self-transcend.

The evolving mystic is involved in an ongoing creation story – of him/herself and of the cultures s/he inhabits. I have offered the orientation and some preliminary practices to facilitate this evolving narrative of our personal and collective lives. As we embrace this evolving journey, we do so on behalf of and as the universe itself, in human form and consciousness. It is my contention that Christianity, which finds itself in a crisis of decline, will need to embrace explicitly the paradigm of evolution which is the gift of science, but which is not limited to the physical realm.

Ingram Content Group UK Ltd.
Milton Keynes UK
UKHW021951080523
421401UK00015B/905